The Essential Guide to
Successful School Trips

The Essential Guide to Successful School Trips

John Trant

Longman
is an imprint of

Harlow, England • London • New York • Boston • San Francisco • Toronto • Sydney • Singapore • Hong Kong
Tokyo • Seoul • Taipei • New Delhi • Cape Town • Madrid • Mexico City • Amsterdam • Munich • Paris • Milan

PEARSON EDUCATION LIMITED

Edinburgh Gate
Harlow CM20 2JE
United Kingdom
Tel: +44 (0)1279 623623
Fax: +44 (0)1279 431059
Website: www.pearsoned.co.uk

First published in Great Britain in 2010

© Pearson Education Limited 2010

Pearson Education is not responsible for the content of third party internet sites.

ISBN: 978-1-4082-0447-4

British Library Cataloguing-in-Publication Data
A CIP catalogue record for this book can be obtained from the British Library

Library of Congress Cataloging-in-Publication Data
Trant, John.
    The essential guide to successful school trips / John Trant.
        p. cm.
    Includes index.
    ISBN 978-1-4082-0447-4 (pbk.)
    1. School field trips. 2. Education, Elementary--Activity programs. 3. Students--Travel.
    4. Education--Standards. 5. Travel. I. Title.
        LB1047.T73 2010
        371.3'84--dc22
                        2010009678

10 9 8 7 6 5 4 3 2 1
14 13 12 11 10

Set by 3
Printed in Great Britain by Henry Ling Ltd., at the Dorset Press, Dorchester, Dorset

Dedicated to the memory of Jo and Wyn and the future of Lucy and Diana

Contents

About the author

John Trant first developed an interest in trips and expeditions as a cadet in the Air Training Corps where he took part in regular camps in the UK, Cyprus and Gibraltar. As a 17-year-old Cadet Sergeant, he planned and led his first overnight exercise and subsequently developed an interest in leadership. While working in his first teaching post John trained as a mountain leader and took charge of the Duke of Edinburgh's Award at the school, leading Silver and Gold expeditions in mountainous country. He then became an Alpine Ski Leader and continues to run regular ski trips to Europe and North America.

John studied Design & Technology and Education at Brunel University followed by an MA in Art and Design in Education at London University's Institute of Education, where he gained further insight into the power of museums and galleries in the teaching of art and design. Most recently he completed an MEd in Educational Leadership and School Improvement at the University of Cambridge, where he researched informal teacher learning during school field trips.

John has taught Design & Technology, Art and IT in maintained and independent schools in the UK and Australia and is currently head of D&T at an independent senior school in Hertfordshire.

Author's Acknowledgements

This book might never have been written were it not for the inspirational influence of the Educational Leadership and School Improvement team at the University of Cambridge, particularly my research supervisor Sue Swaffield. My colleagues there, and at my school, have been a constant source of counsel and inspiration and have provided so many fascinating stories and anecdotes, some of which appear in this book. To the many colleagues from schools up and down the country whom I've only met through correspondence, I'm grateful for sharing their tales of professional challenge during school trips of all kinds.

I am also grateful to the authors of the many sources and references used in this book, for their contributions to the literature in the substantive area of education outside the classroom and educational practice more broadly.

My wife Diana has been the most constant source of encouragement and support during the development of this book and deserves my eternal appreciation and thanks.

Publisher's acknowledgements

We are grateful to the following for permission to reproduce copyright material:

'Costs for school activities' from www.directgov.uk and 'Statistics on drug-taking' from www.dh.gov; Crown copyright material is reproduced with the permission of the Controller of HMSO and the Queen's Printer for Scotland; Definitions of leadership in Chapter 4 from 'The Alphabet Soup of Leadership', *Inform Leadership for Learning* (MacBeath, J., 2003); The General Teaching Council for England for extract from GTC Code of Conduct (p136, Chapter 5); extract on p159 from *Expedition Guide*, Duke of Edinburgh's Award (Keay, W.), 2000; 'Parents demand answers after children escape Stortford bus blaze', E. Reeve, 16 March 2009, with permission from *Herts & Essex Observer*.

Every effort has been made by the publisher to obtain permission from the appropriate source to reproduce material which appears in this book. In some instances we may have been unable to trace the owners of copyright material and would appreciate any information that would enable us to do so.

Introduction

Like many education professionals I have always been fascinated by the way children change their behaviour when learning out of school. Different rules seem to apply when the structure and fabric of the school building are no longer present. Children seem to communicate differently and to adopt a more fluid style of learning. There has always been something special about the school trip and many of our fondest memories of school seem to be rooted in this unusual experience of learning. As a teacher I have seen how children adopt different personas beyond the school gates; they seem somehow more human and interesting when they are in the 'real world', beyond the contrived confines of a classroom. Learning in the 'real world' seems to bring about a change and a more personalised way of learning, whether it be about the structure of sand dunes on a geography field trip, or about their own sense of social capital and confidence during a language exchange. Learning away from school – because of its special nature – can be most powerful.

My own experience of education outside the classroom (EOtC) or, as it is now known, *learning* outside the classroom (the DCSF likes regularly to change names) has taken place in museums, art galleries, factories, universities, sculpture parks, workshops, during expeditions and on ski slopes. The power of these places of learning always impresses me and humbles my own skills as a teacher. Children seem to develop a sense of place in terms of their own learning and social development on these occasions that some might argue is stifled in the normal school environment. The current government has recognised the value of LOtC and in 2006 produced a manifesto to lay out its plans for improving the education of children of all ages as part of the Every Child Matters policy and following the Extended Schools Initiative in 2005. Recognising the power of learning opportunities beyond the classroom is an important step towards a truly meaningful school curriculum, but the responsibility for delivering these opportunities in a supportive way is down to us, the classroom teachers.

It is my, and my colleagues', experience of these various types of trips at home and abroad that led me to think about their planning and organisation and the potential for personal and professional development while on them. From a teacher's perspective, many of the events that are experienced while on a school trip seem to be heightened or exaggerated due to the distance away from the school base. While away on a trip, particularly a foreign one, a teacher can be faced with a myriad of decisions and dilemmas that a team of colleagues would generally deal with under normal circumstances in school. When you're out, you're on your own! OK, maybe it's not that bad, but there is a sense of separation. I remember taking my first trip and feeling a huge sense of responsibility for the children in my care – if something went wrong it was down to me to sort it out; there was no immediate support system to hand to deal with it for me. As a recently qualified teacher that feeling was liberating – no SMT around to fall back on, and the success would be all mine to relish if I did a good job. The result was truly empowering. Since then I've been involved in a wide range of trips and educational experiences away from school and have enjoyed every single one, almost. But what if something does go wrong, what would I do and how would I cope?

Many educational leadership Masters degree courses and one-day CPD courses look at 'dilemmas' from a leadership perspective – issues or events that crop up that need someone to take a decision. While enjoying a challenging discussion on a range of scenarios with colleagues on my recent Masters course, it occurred to me that there are many dilemmas faced by teachers that are specific to school trips. Dilemmas which aren't merely exercises or role-play opportunities, but real ones that require action. This book, therefore, is a blend of two aspects of essential educational practice – 'planning school educational trips' and 'dealing with dilemmas or problems'.

Before continuing, we need to establish what a school trip is and what constitutes education outside the classroom. As with many types of educational activity, trips and EOtC are intended to lead to academic or social development. But we are specifically interested in those activities where teachers or youth workers and volunteer leaders can have some input, take a leadership role and provide a supportive structure to help and encourage learning and development in a location more suited to dealing with the key topic of interest. A trip like this will be made when the traditional mix of classroom, textbook and teacher just isn't good enough. Often you will lead a trip to add contextual detail to a theoretical issue being discussed in class, such as a geography investigation into regeneration in the inner cities – much better if you can actually see it – or a primary school trip to a natural history museum, where a class project on dinosaurs can be given more impact.

Education outside the classroom *does not* mean opening the doors and moving tables outside to carry on in your normal pedagogic style. EOtC is more about thinking about your teaching and realising that powerful learning experiences can happen beyond the classroom. In this book it is used as an umbrella term to cover a range of activities and trips. So much of what is learnt by teachers from taking pupils on a trip to the zoo can be applied to a ski trip or a French exchange – there's just so much cross-over. EOtC can take place within your school grounds, but we really need to think about how we use space and facilities, and how we present to the class and interact with it.

In order to provide a sense of what sort of trips and activities might constitute EotC, I have categorised some of the different types broadly as follows, but this is by no means an exhaustive list – feel free to add to it.

Residential and expeditions – academic, social, physical and leisure, normally two or more days in length.

Residential field studies

Language exchanges

Ski trips, diving trips or similar

Music and art tours

Outdoor pursuits (e.g. Duke of Edinburgh's Award expeditions)

Sports tours

Curriculum focused – normally one day in length.

Libraries

Museums and galleries

Zoos

Farm visits

Theatre productions and concerts

Industrial visits

Seminars, workshops and conferences

Day field studies (e.g. geography central business district surveys)

Children's universities

Study support

Almost anything can fit into the criteria for a school trip or, more broadly, EOtC. Below, I suggest some success criteria that might be helpful when thinking about a trip or an opportunity for EOtC.

- **Make it different**. Don't waste the trip or go to the trouble of going out into the school grounds if what you're going to do can be just as easily covered in class. Plan for your trip to stick in the memory of your pupils for all the right reasons. Also, consider your own teaching – it'll need to be different from your normal classroom practice to be truly effective.

- **Make it count**. Have your learning objectives organised before you go. A sports tour can have social and physical learning objectives, a museum trip could have analytical and interpretation objectives. Don't go without objectives.

- **Use it**. Use the trip/EOtC experience when you come back to school. Never leave it as a stand-alone event.

Learning away from school can be extremely powerful. If given room and time, children can become more independent and confident learners able to deal with the world around them in an intelligent and critical manner. Our job as teachers is to allow this to happen but to guide and provide structure and safety where necessary.

A thinking routine

While reading this book it might help to organise your thinking in a more structured way. One way of doing this is to use a thinking routine. Thinking routines are just a way of organising your reactions to new information or experiences. The routine that many colleagues find helpful and easy to remember is the 'connect–extend–challenge' routine, developed as part of Harvard University's 'Project Zero'.

Connect

What is it about what you've read or experienced that you connect with? Have you had a similar experience and dealt with it in the same way? Does the new information prompt you to think about your experience in a different way?

Extend

Does this information or experience encourage you to extend your knowledge, change your practice or develop in some way? By extend we mean improve, develop – move on.

Challenge

Does the information or experience encourage you to challenge what you do, or do you know better? Can you challenge what's written? Does it challenge your idea of best practice? Does it challenge you to change?

You can get more information about this excellent teaching project via the Project Zero website: (www.pz.harvard.edu/vt)

These routines are just one idea presented in this book to help you to think about your own practice. You're encouraged to add your own notes in the margin (unless this is a library copy, of course) and to discuss the contents with your colleagues in your professional learning communities. By doing so, you will contribute to the developing knowledge on this interesting area of professional practice. Better still, if you have any interesting anecdotes or thoughts to share, do get in touch (email: jhtrant1973@yahoo.co.uk).

Before you go: preparation and planning

Establishing a rationale

What this chapter will explore:

- Why go on school trips?
- What barriers are there to overcome, and what opportunities exist?
- What are the academic, intellectual and practical benefits of school trips?
- How can school trips contribute to the development of social capital?
- What common school trip problems should teachers be aware of?

This chapter will provide an overview of recent thinking on learning outside the classroom and will explore the various associated conflicts and opportunities. In this chapter and those that follow you will be invited to reflect on your own experience. You will see some invitations to 'Reflect on practice' at strategic points, but don't feel restricted to consider these issues alone. Hopefully this chapter will encourage reflection on school trips and maybe your practice more generally. I've tried to include references that might help to give an indication of the developing academic research in the area too. This is to underline the importance of learning outside the classroom as a key component of school improvement strategies. Getting children, parents and teachers to understand that learning can occur anywhere, not just in the traditional classroom, is a major goal that many of us share and a philosophy that, together with theoretical perspectives surrounding informal and social learning, underpin this book.

Why go on school trips?

School trips are memorable events

If you think back to your own school days, often one of the most memorable experiences you'll have had will have been on a trip or visit. The nature of being away from school heightens the senses and really sticks in the memory – it's something out of the ordinary routine. I can remember our first year (year 7 now) history trip to Dover and Deal castles as if it were yesterday, and I can also remember the reason that the whole year group was banned from further trips – nothing at all to do with me of course! Nevertheless, I can still remember most of the history content that we learnt, not to mention lessons about how to behave!

Trips and visits are special times for your pupils and also for young developing teachers. In his book *The SAS Guide to Teaching*, Carline (2006) gives a fairly cynical assessment of the school trip, citing union advice and the hassle of risk assessments and health and safety concerns as good reasons for not getting involved. Each to their own of course, and these may be issues that you and your colleagues have discussed in the past. But, if these barriers are truly preventing you from planning a school trip, then I think you and your pupils are missing out.

School trips encourage an appreciation of social learning in the real world

I think, and hope, you agree that learning shouldn't just take place in the classroom, rather it should happen anywhere and at any time: on the bus to school; on a museum or gallery visit; a ski trip or rugby tour; even while watching TV. There should be no restrictions to where and how children and young adults can learn. There are big issues to overcome, however. I'm not naive enough to suggest that we should all leap out into the wilderness or cram all our learning into museums and galleries, and I know that not all schools and parents have the same facility to cover the costs involved. Of course there are other issues involved, not least of which is the ogre of health and safety, but as I hope you'll see in Chapter 2 the dreaded risk assessment can be a useful tool for reflective professional development and help prepare for future school inspections.

Perhaps the biggest hurdle we face as teachers is getting children to understand that they have the capacity to learn through their own volition. Once they have learnt 'how to learn' they can really start to develop their intellect and social confidence, or what can also be described as intellectual and social capital (see Schuller *et al.*, 2004).

School trips are good for teachers too

I organise trips because they are primarily great fun. They are fantastic opportunities for you and your pupils to interact in a different environment. For many pupils, seeing their teachers as learners, human beings even, can be a powerful epiphany. To see their teacher as a learner again gives them a positive role model. We often view learners and teachers as members of different tribes (them and us) in the classroom. This makes it difficult for you, the teacher, to be seen as a proper role model, as you are always in opposition to the other tribe. Your pupils won't all seek careers in teaching, so why do we expect them to see us as academic role models unless we exhibit good learning skills ourselves too?

The best teachers seem to infect kids with their enthusiasm for learning, and the school trip allows greater exposure of teachers to their pupils during a concentrated time period. A day's focused science discovery in a science museum with an enthusiastic and encouraging teacher must surely have an impact that is greater than sitting through a week's worth of 35-minute lessons. Of course, some teachers are perhaps not suited to taking trips at all, as a certain type of relaxed authority is needed for a leader of a school trip. So it's not for everyone, but as I'll continue to argue, the trip, or any kind of education outside the classroom (EOtC), can be a powerful and effective tool for lifelong learning. Research on the issue of learning outside the classroom (LOtC), although still in its early stages, is growing thanks to the likes of Hunter-Jones, Kisiel, Anderson and Zhang, Maynard and Waters, and Falk and Dierking, all of whom are working to understand this phenomenon from a variety of perspectives in many different school settings around the world.

What barriers are there to overcome, and what opportunities exist?

Barriers

Recently, a number of government hearings (Education and Skills Committee 2005 and Constitutional Affairs Committee 2006), an OFSTED report (2008) and a manifesto on 'learning outside the classroom' (DfES, 2006) have raised the profile of school trips following concerns over their possible demise. While resoundingly favourable, they recognise that barriers to, and negative aspects of, school trips do exist and might include: the disruption to the school day or other subject lessons; the proliferation of examinations in January and June in the UK; inertia in experienced teachers who have seen 'fads' come and go; cost; risk; and advice from teaching unions to avoid non-contractual educational visits.

In a recent survey of geography teachers by Parry and Clarke (2004), '62 per cent of those questioned agreed or strongly agreed that geography teachers were deterred from organising field trips because of the threat of legal action' (p231). Most recently, in a 2008 OFSTED report, 'poor behaviour; logistical difficulties, including the large numbers of pupils involved; disruption to the timetable; cost; health and safety issues and cultural barriers' were cited by senior leaders as challenges to engaging in geography fieldwork in schools that were not meeting the statutory standards (p42). Maynard and Waters (2007) echo this, noting that some of the respondents in their research into LOtC in early years schools in Wales were 'worried about the possibility of litigation in the event of a child being hurt' (p259).

Taking the health and safety barrier as an example, I wonder on what basis some of these schools and teachers are making their decisions. Of the thousands of school trips taking place each year only a very small number result in any sort of accident or incident. In fact, between 2001 and 2006 only 18 fatalities and 519 non-fatal injuries, relatively small numbers nationally, occurred to children between the ages of one and 15 as a result of activities in education, training, research and recreation/sport (Health and Safety Executive Statistics 0916).

Perhaps the concern or obsession for health and safety is media driven. The Health and Safety Executive (HSE) has long been blamed for restricting schools with red tape but is it their fault, or ours, that we have formed this negative opinion?

> 'All too often "health and safety" is blamed for imposing unjustifiable bureaucracy on teachers ... As a regulator, the HS[C] wants to see risks managed sensibly and responsibly, not eliminated.'

> (Hackitt, 2007, web press release)

Despite reassurance and encouragement via a number of government sources (*Every Child Matters*, 2004; *Learning Outside the Classroom Manifesto*, 2006;

OFSTED report on *Geography in Schools*, 2008), there remains concern that safety and litigation are genuine barriers to progress.

Turning risk and red tape to your advantage

It could be that some barriers might be lessened by embedding new legislation and policy (Compensation Act 2006; Every Child Matters, 2004; and Learning Outside the Classroom, 2006). Indeed, despite the real and imagined barriers discussed above, health and safety red tape and legislation could actually provide a framework to get things right and improve 'the school experience'. By developing a discourse on safety, and the pedagogy of LOtC, teachers can reflect on possibilities and opportunities rather than barriers.

In an effort to provide further reassurance and clarity on how litigation and compensation can be sought and against whom, the UK government introduced the Compensation Act 2006. The Act recognises that there is value in activities, such as school field trips, that have inherent but acceptable risks, if they provide 'social utility'. The law is sympathetic towards teachers trying to do the right thing, so this should be seen as an opportunity to develop LOtC and related diverse pedagogy rather than shy away from it.

This book tries to present barriers such as risk and poor behaviour as opportunities to get together with colleagues and generate knowledge about our profession and our practice. I see no reason to avoid school trips if we have the support of our colleagues in schools and interest from the kids.

In summary, the reasons not to go might be articulated as:

● Fear of litigation if something goes wrong

● Expense

● Time 'wasted' that could be spent on actual class teaching

● Disruption of the school day and other colleagues' lessons

● Behavioural problems

● Lack of staff cover for proper ratios

● Ignorance

● The sheer effort involved in organisation and 'paperwork'.

And the reasons to go might be to:

● Vary the learning environment for your pupils

● Expose pupils to a wider range of learning activities and opportunities

● Connect the real world to the curriculum

● Improve awareness of geographical and social differences

● Encourage exploration

- Encourage development of social and intellectual capital
- Improve your own knowledge and skills
- Enjoy something different
- Work with colleagues in new ways
- Develop leadership opportunities for staff.

Of course it's up to you at the end of the day, but I think the reasons to go far outweigh the reasons not to. My advice is to get out there and start learning with the kids!

Reflecting on practice

How does what you've read resonate with your own experience?

Could you add anything to the list of reasons to go or reasons not to go on a school trip?

Is there anything unique about your school or setting that produces specific challenges, barriers or opportunities?

What did you **connect** with?

What might **extend** your thinking or practice?

What **challenged** you?

Much of the current driving force for LOtC comes from the Labour government's Every Child Matters policy (DfES, 2004), which is a development of the 'No Child Left Behind' strategy in the US. Typically, there are a number of strategies, targets, initiatives and policies associated with Every Child Matters that help to frame our understanding of the benefits of LOtC, not least of which is the Extended Schools Initiative (DfES, 2005). While a good deal of resources have been made available recently, notably to set up the Council for Learning Outside the Classroom, more consideration needs to be given to developing LOtC at ITT (Initial Teacher Training) level.

Even a cursory look at Figure 1.1 opposite will give you some idea of the complex relationships involved. But take a step back and essentially the benefits of EOtC/ LOtC can be broken down into two important key benefits that encompass most of the small boxes in green. In the most general possible terms these benefits are:

- Intellectual/practical experience and enrichment
- Social development.

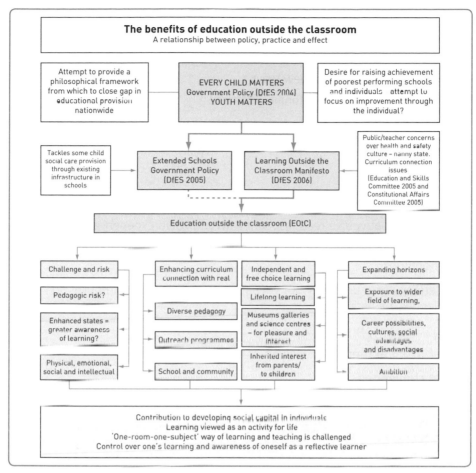

Fig 1.1 The benefits of education outside the classroom.

What are the academic, intellectual and practical benefits of school trips?

'While experience may be the foundation of learning, it does not necessarily lead to it; there needs to be active involvement with it.'

(Boud *et al.*, 1993: 9)

First-hand experience

To benefit from an experience intellectually we need to be aware of its potential for learning – learners need to understand why they are doing what they are doing and be able to shape their experience. Teachers try to encourage pupils to be active all the time – to take notes, make sketches, converse or make models as in a group problem solving exercise. Being involved in the session through a physical connection may make it possible to achieve a greater learning gain because the learner's body has taken part: limbs have moved, blood has flowed, pulse rate changed and neurons stimulated. There is an active connection with what is going on; involvement and connection are central to the experience *and* learning.

Cooper (2006) suggests that adventurous activities, where children climb trees and build dens, satisfy 'an inner need' to learn new physical skills (p23). Skills that once learnt through an active experience can be recalled later in life – the experience informs sustained learning. But without reflection on the experience itself and a review of what is already known by the learner, the transition to true learning cannot take place (see Kolb's learning cycle (1984) and Chapter 2). Reflection and internal cross-checking need to be encouraged in the learner.

If learning through experience via LOtC is to effect reflective, active and joined-up learning the role of the teacher must also be reviewed. The value of an LOtC experience for a pupil could be diminished if teachers are only viewed as 'active transmitters of knowledge' (Collins *et al.*, 2002: 148). In this way learning is almost forced upon the pupil and is not interactive. Collins *et al.* suggest 'opening a conversation with learners' in order that they become part of the development of effective interactive teaching (p149). Teachers need to adapt their practice when away from the classroom.

Enriching classroom learning

Perhaps the pivotal concept of this book, for learners, is that LOtC can add to what happens inside a school classroom by 'enriching' learning. Yet the assumption that pupil performance can be improved by simply experiencing or studying a concept away from the normal school setting is a little naive. Payne and Owen (2006) suggest that there is a problem when considering how the benefits of LOtC can be transferred to other areas of learning and used beneficially. Their study noted a dissonance between activities away from school and those in the classroom. It is difficult for LOtC to have a sustained impact on a child's experience if the lessons learnt can't be transferred elsewhere in the curriculum or even the subject; this is not a problem in study support sessions in the mode of the Extended School, but more so for adventure courses or loosely focused museum visits.

Getting pupils to make connections between practice and theory is perhaps one of the trickiest challenges I face in my own teaching. However, Braund and Reiss (2006) suggest that out-of-school science visits have the capacity to make this easier because they can offer 'more authentic practical experiences' which encourage connection (p219). However, the learning gains probably depend on the design and structure of the experience and so the success of the trip must be context dependent.

Pupils will often ask how a trip relates to a certain examination paper. Some see the school experience purely in terms of grades and examination success, and so to them this way of connecting may be effective. Indeed, some teachers might even question whether trips are worth engaging in at all given the time it takes away from normal lessons. Nevertheless, the educational value of such curriculum-focused trips is widely acknowledged among colleagues and researchers alike, despite some suggesting that the link between classroom and LOtC experience is not always as strong as it could be, as Xanthoudaki, writing in 1998 recognised: 'there is limited incorporation of museum and gallery visits into classroom art practice' (p182). More recent research has noticed similar problems (Kisiel, 2005) and continues to recommend that greater effect can be achieved through more careful planning and a change in teaching style while away from the classroom.

However, enrichment courses that aren't examination focused might give children more space to think about how they learn, and provide opportunity for reflection as Hany and Grosch postulate:

'Even short encounters with peers who have the same interests, passions, and intellectual levels can positively influence gifted adolescents' self concept, peer status, or life goals.'

(Hany and Grosch, 2007: 522)

Feedback from my own pupils who have attended 'Headstart' or 'Smallpeice Trust' residential taster courses at university engineering departments, for example, would certainly support this suggestion and hint at wider benefits than improved examination performance. Indeed, many of the stories they tell about friendships formed during group work sessions and challenges add weight to my claim that social development can take place during trips too. The type of social development taking place is most often referred to as 'social capital'.

How can school trips contribute to the development of social capital?

Social capital theory describes how a variety of social factors might influence, or build, a person's capacity to gain from social experiences. It is the facility that allows people to absorb – via membership of social groups, access to networks of friendship or support and trust and reciprocity – the negative or challenging things that happen to them. Having social capital can mean that one might have 'people one can turn to in a crisis' (MacBeath *et al.*, 2007: 42), or a strong support network among one's peers when engaged in homework.

Briefly, there are three types of social capital of interest here, they are: bonding social capital (close networks with similar people providing protective resources and reciprocity); bridging social capital (wider networks of different people providing productive resources); and linking social capital (a type of bridging but on a vertical axis with hierarchical structures, e.g. student and teacher linking) (Stevens *et al.*, 2007).

Allied to the concept of social capital is that of 'intellectual capital', which is a key element in the development of a person's sense of worth or self-efficacy. These various capitals are built through positive and negative social, intellectual and emotional experiences. The broader a person's experience of life, people and the world around them, the greater the opportunity to build social capital.

One of the most established mechanisms for developing general social awareness in young people is the Duke of Edinburgh's Award Scheme. The handbook for the expeditions section of the Award lists ten benefits to young people:

> *'The expeditions section should provide opportunities to: demonstrate enterprise; work as a member of a team; respond to a challenge; develop self reliance; develop leadership skills; recognise strengths in others; make decisions and accept the consequences; plan and execute a task; reflect on personal performance; and enjoy and appreciate the countryside.'*

> (Keay, 2000: 2–3)

These benefits dovetail nicely into ways of thinking about social capital theory:

> *'In terms of education, there are three distinct ways in which we can think about the role of social capital: as a vehicle of learning, as an outcome of learning and as an element of the learning context. Perhaps most obviously social capital can be seen as a vehicle of individual learning and personal development.'*

> (Stevens *et al.*, 2007: 2)

So the benefits of the Duke of Edinburgh's Award Scheme could be seen as vehicles, as outcomes and as elements of the learning context.

Bridging social capital may be effected by going to museums and art galleries, or playing sport with people not in your immediate or 'bonded' group, thus extending your network. Having access to a wider network through extra-curricular activities or LOtC might also be beneficial in opening pupils' eyes to the wider world. This strikes a chord with the Extended Schools Initiative, as Stevens *et al.* again report:

'Through extended services, schools can promote activities that build collaborative inter-group relationships between different social groups; and create closer relationships between staff, students, their parents and families.'

(Stevens *et al.*, 2007: 104)

Thus social capital, as a development process and an outcome, sits at the heart of the Every Child Matters policy. It is important to understand that an individual's social capital can change with time and so is not an accurate yardstick with which to evaluate a particular policy or initiative; rather it might be a contributing factor to differing levels of performance or outcome. However, when social capital is high, outcomes may also be high:

'In general, levels of social capital are strongly associated with students' sociopsychological resources, particularly their self-concept of ability. Previous research indicates that this measure is positively related to beneficial educational outcomes.'

(Stevens *et al.*, 2007: 102)

Could it be, therefore, that successful LOtC in the form of a year group geography field trip might provide enough social capital – bonding with established networks, bridging with new colleagues on group tasks and linking with teachers for an extended period of time – to effect a more positive outcome in an individual pupil's examination or piece of coursework than would have been possible before? A question that presents opportunity for further research rather than a straightforward yes or no answer.

Reflecting on practice

Social capital is an extremely interesting area that you may never have come across formally before.

While thinking about the 'connect–extend–challenge' questions, also consider your own childhood at this point:

● Can you recall any instances in your own education that might have been pivotal in developing your own social capital?

● How could you encourage such opportunities for your own pupils?

Conclusion

Establishing a reason to go and understanding the benefits and risks are important thought processes to go through before you even start to plan your activity or think about how you will get there. Without having a rationale and giving thought to your planning and objectives, your trip will be wasted. There is much that you will have read in this chapter that you can debate and disagree with, but the principle that good trips require good planning and leadership is probably not an issue for debate. In Chapter 2 I look at planning the trip and leadership issues that may arise. Rather than go into specific school trip pedagogy in the planning of particular activities for different age groups, I look at organisational systems for framing such activities that you are best suited to planning yourself – you know your pupils better than I, so your planning will reflect this. Consider the advice given in the following chapter as a scaffold for organising your trip and leading your staff and pupils. Before you move on to the next chapter, though, consider the following.

An invitation to reframe your thinking

There are two groups of people who might benefit from a school trip – pupils and teachers.

There are untapped opportunities for teachers to learn from school trips and develop skills and pedagogic techniques: observing others at work; trying different group management tactics; employing different resources; engaging in specialised training; improving subject knowledge; and the often overlooked chance to lead other colleagues.

Also, what about the pupils? What exactly do they think about field trips? This chapter has looked at the reasons why teachers choose to take trips or avoid them. Would your pupils agree? Why not ask them?

Key ideas summary

- There is growing support for school trips and LOtC at national and local government level.
- LOtC is an integral part of the Every Child Matters policy.
- Teachers who take school trips are well supported and protected by unions and the legal system, provided they act professionally.
- Barriers to taking school trips are becoming fewer, and those that exist can be overcome with good collaborative planning.
- Teachers need to adapt their teaching for the different challenges presented by school trips.
- School trips can enrich classroom learning.
- School trips can contribute to social capital development.
- School trips can benefit teachers too by encouraging collaborative planning with colleagues.

Going further

Websites

School trips:

www.hse.gov.uk/schooltrips

For keeping up to date with government documents:

www.publications.parliament.uk

Every Child Matters:

www.dcsf.gov.uk/everychildmatters

OFSTED – for reports into LOtC provision and school trips:

www.ofsted.gov.uk

European Institute of Outdoor Education and Experiential Learning:

www.eoe-network.org

The Institute for Outdoor Learning

www.outdoor-learning.org

The Council for Learning Outside the Classroom:

www.lotc.uk.org

For research on the wider benefits of education:

www.learningbenefits.net

For current social and educational research project information:

www.esrc.ac.uk

Further reading

Andrews, K. (2001) *Extra Learning: New opportunities for the out of school hours* (London: Kogan Page).

Boud, D., Cohen, R. and Walker, D. (1993) Introduction: Understanding Learning from Experience. In Boud, D., Cohen, R. and Walker, D. (eds) *Using Experience for Learning* (Buckingham: Open University Press).

Carline, B. (2006) *The SAS Guide to Teaching* (London: Continuum).

Collins, J., Harkin, J. and Nind, M. (2002) *Manifesto for Learning* (London: Continuum).

DfES (2006) *Learning Outside the Classroom Manifesto* (Nottingham: DfES).

DfES (2005) *Extended Schools: Access to opportunities and services for all, a prospectus* (Nottingham: DfES).

DfES (2004) *Every Child Matters: Change for children in schools* (Nottingham: DfES).

Hackitt, J. (2007) Learning to manage risk an essential part of growing up, says HSC *Health and Safety Executive (HSE)* website press release, www.hse.gov.uk/press/2007/c07018.htm?ebul=hsegen/29-oct-2007&cr=15 (accessed 11 December 2007).

Keay, W. (2000) *Expedition Guide* (Wellingborough: Sterling Press).

Kolb, D. (1984) *Experiential Learning: Experience as the source of learning and development* (Englewood Cliffs, NJ: Prentice-Hall).

Moon, J. (2004) *A Handbook of Reflective and Experiential Learning* (London: RoutledgeFalmer).

National Commission on Education (1996) *Success Against the Odds: Effective schools in disadvantaged areas* (London: Routledge).

Schuller, T., Preston, J., Hammond, C., Brasset-Grundy, A. and Bynner, J. (2004) *The Benefits of Learning: The impact on health, family life and social capital* (London: RoutledgeFalmer).

TDA (2008) *QTS Standards Guidance* (London: TDA).

Relevant research studies

Anderson, D. and Zhang, Z. (2003) Teacher Perceptions of Field-Trip Planning and Implementation, *Visitor Studies Today*, 6 (3), 6–11.

Cooper, G. (2006) Disconnected Children, *Horizons Magazine* (Institute of Outdoor Learning), spring 2006, issue 33, 22–25.

Braund, M. and Reiss, M. (2006) Validity and Worth in the Science Curriculum: Learning school science outside the laboratory, *The Curriculum Journal*, 17 (3), 213–228.

Falk, J. and Dierking, L. (1997) School Field Trips: Assessing their long-term impact (courtesy of Falk, J.H. personal collection, pp1–14); also published in *Curator: The Museum Journal*, 40 (3), 211–218.

Falk, J., Moussouri, T. and Coulson, D. (1998) The Effect of Visitors' Agendas on Museum Learning, *Curator: The Museum Journal*, 41, 107–120.

Griffin, J. (2007) Students, Teachers, and Museums: Toward an intertwined learning circle. In: Falk, J. H., Dierking, L. D. and Foutz, S. (eds) *In Principle, In Practice* (Lanham: Altamira).

→

Griffin, J. (1994) Learning to Learn in Informal Settings, *Research in Science Education*, 24, 121–128.

Hany, E. and Grosch, C. (2007) Long-Term Effects of Enrichment Summer Courses on the Academic Performance of Gifted Adolescents, *Educational Research and Evaluation*, 13 (6), 521–537.

Hunter-Jones, J. (2006) The Compensation Act 2006 and School Trips, *Education 3–13*, 34 (3), 223–232.

Kendell, S., Murfield, J., Dillon, J. and Wilkin, A. (2006) *Education Outside the Classroom: Research to identify what training is offered by initial teacher training institutions* (Research Report 802) (Nottingham: DfES).

Kisiel, J. (2005) Understanding Elementary Teacher Motivations for Science Fieldtrips, *Science Education*, 89 (6), 936–955.

MacBeath, J., Gray, J., Cullen, J., Frost, D., Steward, S. and Swaffield, S. (2007) *Schools on the Edge: Responding to challenging circumstances* (London: Paul Chapman).

Maynard, T. and Waters, J. (2007) Learning in the Outdoor Environment: A missed opportunity? *Early Years*, 27 (3), 255–265.

OFSTED (2008) *Geography in Schools: Changing practice* (London: OFSTED).

Parry, G. and Clarke, L. (2004) Risk Assessment and Geography Teachers: A survey, *Education and the Law*, 16 (2–3), 115–131.

Payne, J. and Owen, J. (2006) From Transfer to Reconstruction: The process of deploying learning elsewhere, *Horizons Magazine* (Institute of Outdoor Learning), winter 2006, issue 36, 24–27.

Stevens, P., Lupton, R., Mujtaba, T. and Feinstein, L. (2007) *The Development and Impact of Young People's Social Capital in Secondary Schools* (London: Centre for Research on the Wider Benefits of Learning).

Xanthoudaki, M. (1998) Is It Always Worth the Trip? The contribution of museum and gallery education programmes to classroom art education, *Cambridge Journal of Education*, 28 (2), 181–195.

The planning process

What this chapter will explore:

- Considerations when planning your trip
- Your trip, your team, your responsibility – does the buck stop here?
- Your objectives
- Getting down to details
- The risk assessment
- Communication and information
- Inclusion, equality and behaviour

The idea for the trip needs to come from someone first of all, someone who will have the vision and tenacity to drive it forward. However, one person can't do everything; there must be a distribution of leadership right from the start. This doesn't mean delegating each task to different people and doing nothing yourself. It means working collaboratively towards a common goal by using individual skills, strengths and knowledge inherent in your team.

Your trip, your team, your responsibility – does the buck stop here?

Many see leadership as a collaborative activity which involves expertise being sourced from a collegial group of professionals who have a shared goal and focus. Having said that, old-fashioned definitions of responsibility, in law and in educational management, still call for a responsible figurehead: someone who will take responsibility for the whole trip. That's all very well and good, but it doesn't properly reflect the nature of what you do and how you and your colleagues most often behave when on school trips. In reality we tend to discuss major decisions and come to a consensus, or even a compromise when needed.

So who's in your team and how many staff do you need?

Who makes up your team depends on what you see as your aims and objectives for the venture you are embarking on. In the case of a biology field trip, your team would almost certainly be made up of colleagues in your department, or interested staff members who are making up a suitable staff/pupil ratio. At times this ratio can be a difficult thing to achieve. In a small subject department in a senior school, the burden of responsibility for trips can be quite high, particularly in subjects that rely heavily on field trips as part of their teaching strategy such as geography and biology. Imagine a biology department with two teaching staff, both of whom have decided to take their classes to a local science centre for a programme of enrichment. Each class has approximately 30 children, so there is no way that they can manage to take 60 children between them and satisfy the DCSF's required staff/pupil ratio of 1:15–20. They'll have to take extra staff. This can be where the problems start.

Supervision

Your school may have its own policy on supervision but the DCSF's guidelines, although quite old now, are the best place to start. They suggest the following ratios:

- 1 adult for every 6 pupils in years 1–3 (under fives should have a higher ratio).

- 1 adult for every 10–15 pupils in years 4–6.

- 1 adult for every 10–20 pupils from year 7 onwards.

(Adventurous trips and trips near water may require higher ratios and specialist staff with appropriate training, so the above ratios may need to be reviewed for your activity. Remember, these are minimum standards.)

In an ideal school staffroom, you'd just approach staff from other classes or subjects for some help. Obviously there would be lesson cover issues to be resolved, you'd also have to make a deposit in the 'favour bank' for later on, and you would need to make sure that the staff you took weren't always the same people: goodwill can wear out. All of these relatively simple negotiations require what is so often rather blandly referred to as 'good people skills'. Being able to deal sensitively, fairly and sympathetically with colleagues must surely be a key aspect of educational leadership, and so planning a trip surely must contribute to your profile as a leader. You may not be in an actual 'position of authority' in the usual sense, say a head of department, head of year or senior manager, but that doesn't stop you from leading colleagues from time to time – what Peter Gronn (2000) and James Spillane (2006) refer to as 'distributed leadership'.

Why not try this?

Delegate tasks such as collecting consent forms and compiling medical or special needs data sheets to the trip staff.

But also:

Distribute leadership roles such as setting trip discipline policy or leading the teaching of a unit, delivery of an activity or chairing a collaboration meeting on learning objectives.

Whether you delegate tasks or distribute leadership roles will depend on the unique skills that each member of your team can bring to the trip. However, there will be some tasks and duties that you can't avoid. In Figure 2.1 I suggest a way of thinking about and organising some of the common duties and responsibilities involved in running a school trip.

In an ideal world you get the help you need. But often there are many internal tensions and 'issues' among colleagues, and this means that teachers tend to have a relatively small 'pool' from which to select help when they need it.

When planning an educational activity that you have a belief in and a passion for, you need a team that you can work with and who share your passion. So what are your options if you can't get the help you need? Teachers who work in infant and junior schools are expert at engaging the extremely useful help of parents and grandparents in chaperoning trips out. These helpers tend to be interested and enthusiastic and are normally very happy to be asked on a regular basis. Many schools have a rota system which parents can sign up to, so that the load is spread among the parent body.

Classroom teaching assistants can also contribute a great deal, particularly as they have such a good knowledge of the children in the first place. We mustn't forget that there are benefits for the helpers too. Parents achieve a greater under-

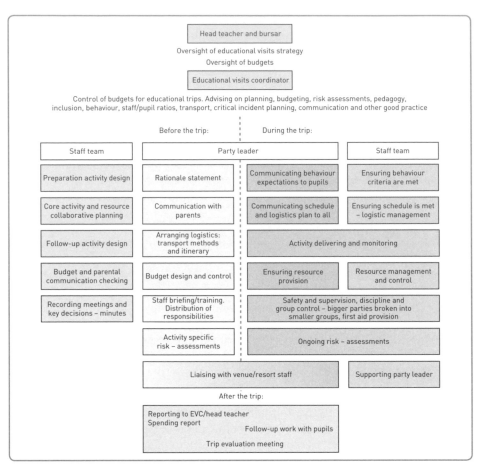

Fig 2.1: Distribution and delegation of duties

standing of their child's learning, behaviour and development when they engage in such activities. They also develop a better understanding of what it is to be a teacher. In some cases parents who help develop an interest in education again: attend night classes, take part-time degrees or even join the ranks of trainee teachers. Above all, a sense of being part of the school community and making a contribution seem to be strong motivating factors:

> *'I love helping at the school, particularly in my son's class where we can give tuition with reading and sums, but the most fun are the trips out. You see the teachers, mums and children behaving in different ways; it's so much fun and really memorable.'*

> (Infant school mum)

There is a problem though: the CRB (Criminal Records Bureau) check. How do you ensure the safety of the children you are taking on a trip, while avoiding huge expense for your school and paperwork for you? Adults who work or volunteer with children on a regular basis should be checked for a criminal record. There are extremely good reasons for this and, unfortunately, the risk of not checking is just too great. Of course, you also risk alienating and upsetting well-meaning and genuine parents and friends who just want to help out. As with many things, you need to make sure that you have done the right thing and followed the protocols set down by your employer. I can't stress enough just how important it is to do things by the book here. Unfortunately this whole issue can undermine trust to some extent and is an area that needs sensitive handling.

What about taking your family along too?

Overseas and residential trips are slightly different from day trips in that you'll be spending time away from your own family, often during school holidays. It is tempting to see some school trips as a holiday for all concerned, including the staff. In my experience this idea could not be further from the truth. Ski trips, sports tours and outward bound courses offer great opportunities for pupils to develop skills and social capital, while adults provide the much-needed support (often emotional) and structure. The aim is to provide a safe and enjoyable experience for all. Naturally, there will be moments for relaxation and enjoyment along with the responsibility of the trip, but most of all you're there to work, not play.

Many commercial tour operators who deal with school parties have caught on to the fact that trips are hard for staff with families who get left behind. Many now offer reduced rate family places for the tour leader so that there might be more of an incentive to go. While I'm not against family members coming along on longer trips, I think the concept of reduced cost or even free places can cause some bad feeling. If your family is going to work as part of your team, do evening duties, hospital trips and other tasks, then they'll earn their place. But if they are just along for the ride, you have to question the ethics of their involvement, especially if other trip staff have left their own families at home. I'd be tempted to ignore such offers and keep the family separate from the trip if at all possible. In the case of a critical incident, as tour party leader your loyalties would be divided: look after the pupils, or concentrate on your own family? It's difficult sometimes when running such trips to leave the family at home, but it's the professional thing to do. When you are the leader of a school party, you are responsible to the parents for the safety and wellbeing of their most precious and deeply loved children, and so you must take this extreme honour seriously.

Taking pupils' parents along too?

Taking pupils' parents with you on a sports tour or overseas trip? Trip leaders that I've spoken to are divided on this issue. Some suggest that taking parents is an unnecessary complication: parents can blur the boundaries of supervision responsibility and pupil behaviour expectation and can unintentionally interfere with your leadership. Others suggest that parents who have particular expertise can be valuable on trips, lending helpful further support. But again, there are issues of child protection inherent in taking unchecked personnel on your trip. The simple answer to this dilemma for me has always been to keep trips to staff only.

Former pupils

On some trips I've taken former pupils. On two recent ski trips I took two old boys who had particular skills that I wanted to take advantage of: one, a ski instructor; and the other, an accident and emergency doctor at that time. In both cases the strategy worked well as they had an excellent knowledge of the context of the pupils, given that they'd been pupils at the same school, and were able to relate well to the children in our charge, while adopting a professional distance and gelling well with the staff team. Before you panic about CRB checks, think carefully about the role you expect the individual to take on and how much unsupervised contact you expect them to have.

Reflecting on practice

Building a team relies on common motivations and a shared vision. It is important to communicate this at the early planning stages of a trip. Are people keen to join for the right reasons? Or are you struggling to fill staff places because of misinformation?

Whoever you take will have a significant impact on your trip – try to ensure it is a good one!

A thoroughly professional perspective

Choosing your team is pretty tricky, so a good deal of thought needs to go into this. It may come down to taking the same team you've always taken – it's often a very effective solution and everyone knows what they are doing. This is tempting because it feels like a well-oiled machine when you have a good, tightly knit and knowledgeable team. Nevertheless, it's important to keep your trips inclusive to pupils and staff. You can too easily create a staffroom subgroup or clique by passively refusing entry to others. By doing what you've always done it's surprisingly easy to overlook other talented staff from around the common room.

Newly qualified teachers are often very keen to get involved in activities beyond their own teaching subject, offering enthusiasm, energy and new perspectives and ideas on pedagogy. The probationary year is a pretty busy one, though, so don't expect too much of beginning teachers who are just getting to grips with their new career. However, I'm a strong believer in involving young staff in a range of teaching and learning activities beyond the classroom. In these environments beginning teachers can interact with pupils in different and informal learning environments and even improve their own subject knowledge in the process. As a trip or tour leader you also have a responsibility to set a professional example and to bring these young staff on, and to encourage their own professionalism.

Building a team – criteria

Availability

Surely this has to be your first question: 'Who's available?' If a colleague could really help you with your trip and you value their experience, friendship or expertise, try to make arrangements for their lessons to be covered, or rearrange the trip. If somebody has a talent you think would add to your venture, then headhunt them.

Expertise

Who has the necessary skills for your trip? If it's a subject based field trip then you'll draw your team from the department staff. If the trip is related to an examination soon to take place you'll probably use the staff that teach those groups. But don't discount other members of staff who don't teach that particular year group or subject. Teachers often have interests and expertise beyond their teaching subject and it's good for young learners to see this in action. In infant and junior school scenarios you'll need staff trained for those year groups and their unique needs. For special educational needs scenarios you'll need staff trained in the care of young learners who may need help moving from place to place.

Trust

No doubt about it, whether you're planning an ascent of the Eiger or a visit to a local museum, you need a team you can trust to do the right thing, set the right example, care for your pupils and support you. Some teachers run trips year in, year out with exactly the same team each time, because they know they can trust their colleagues to do what needs doing, often without giving it any thought.

Personality and temperament

We all know teachers who put pupils on edge. These teachers don't help when you're out in public with children, no matter how expert they may be. I've tended to avoid such people when I can. You want cool, relaxed but alert people on your trip, and you need to set the tone yourself, making it clear how you want the trip to go. If you're not an extrovert you might feel it is difficult to do this, but it should not preclude you from a position of leadership. You can use other strategies to help make your trip a success, such as team discussion prior to taking the trip, where the aims and objectives can be collaboratively arrived at and the tone set early on.

Motivation and dedication

Some trips present an attractive opportunity for staff to travel to exotic and exciting destinations seemingly for free. Expeditions to far-flung corners of the planet, classics trips to Greece and art trips to Florence are all commercially available ventures that provide free places to teachers, often based on a 1:10 ratio. Places for staff in some schools are highly sought after and competition can be surprisingly fierce. Achieving a regular seat on some of the more prestigious trips can be seen as confirmation of your 'arrival' in the staffroom pecking order and lead to some trips being 'closed shops'. Not good!

Your objectives

When considering the type of trip you want to create, you'll naturally want to make everyone aware of your overall aims and objectives. Your staff team will be pivotal in this regard and will help to communicate those shared goals to your pupils. While the overall aims are important to establish as part of a rationale for any trip, it might help to consider the individual objectives more closely when discussing the trip with your staff team and then the pupils. By reaching smaller objectives on a biology field trip, for example – by pupils completing a nature study observation schedule on day one, and then designing an experiment to confirm results on day two – the aim of improving the link between observation and experiment design can be achieved in more manageable chunks. Having an awareness of time is important; by missing out one component of a trip because something overran in the morning, or someone was late, can really impact the whole effect of the trip.

A good way of thinking about achieving the objectives on a trip with the staff team is to consider distributing leadership, where teachers can develop their own tactics for achieving an objective that has been identified through strategic collegial planning. When thinking about your objectives, try not to arbitrarily separate opportunities for teacher learning from the more easily considered learning objectives for your pupils. There is great value in considering how your colleagues might benefit from being involved in the trip too.

> **Why not try this?**
>
> It's well worth considering how you and your colleagues can benefit from the experience you are planning, as well as your pupils. Why not integrate teacher learning into the design of the trip?

Some objectives might be more logistic in nature, such as getting everyone to the station by 7pm, or more broadly following your daily itinerary. Having a timekeeper who keeps things moving can be a real help if you are leading a part of your trip or are concerned with an issue that might have arisen. While everyone can take a part in the leadership of the trip, having agreed specific responsibilities helps to avoid confusion over whose role is whose, and allows your trip to run more smoothly – you'll know that the coach is free of litter at the end of the day, because a member of your team has taken a lead and got the kids to clear up.

Often, in a typically distributive leadership way, teachers on trips do things because they see they need doing, taking responsibility for things as the opportunity arises. This is great, but if you have specific learning objectives these must be agreed well in advance: they can't be dealt with in an opportunistic manner. It might be helpful to reflect on how you will know your trip has been a success by thinking about objectives from different interlocking perspectives, as in Figure 2.2.

Clearly, setting success criteria before you start planning can help to ensure that your planning takes these into account. Invariably, when we plan we try to include too much and our expectations become too high, but engaging in discussion with your colleagues can help bring ambitious ideas back down to earth. Thinking in terms of a system or protocol can help form your idea for the trip (see Figure 2.3).

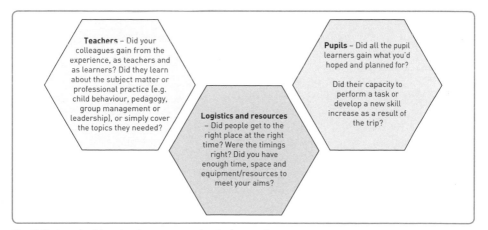

Fig 2.2: Interlocking basic success criteria for a trip

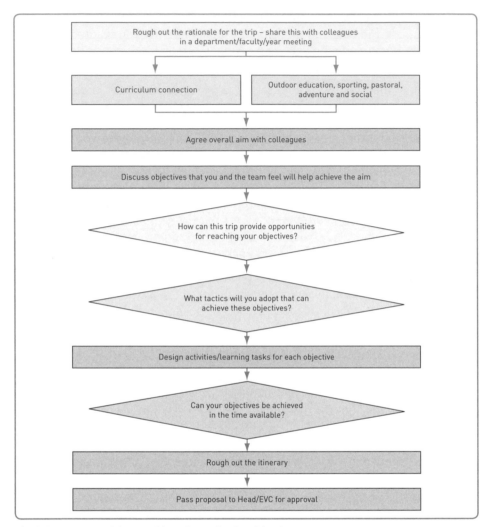

Fig 2.3: A protocol for working through trip objectives

If your trip takes the form of an externally provided workshop, for example, you may need to see how the suggested itinerary and content can link to your aims and objectives.

Getting down to details

There is no point engaging in detailed planning unless the rationale, aims and objectives have been properly thought through. Don't forget that we are interested in all types of trips here, not just academic. You wouldn't start planning in detail for a rock climbing trip until you'd established why you wanted to run it, where it was going and who you were taking. Once all that's out of the way you can get down to the details.

Let's imagine that you've got a set of aims and objectives organised and permission granted to take a trip. Whether it is a day trip or a residential trip you'll need to have some answers ready to some tricky questions. A checklist is best for this and your educational visits coordinator (EVC) might provide you with one. The DfES produced *Health and Safety of Pupils on Educational Trips* back in 1998 and included a planning flowchart to help teachers organise safe visits. I found it a little basic, so I've created a more detailed checklist that can be adapted in any way you want. The checklist below concerns a residential trip specifically, but the principle is the same for shorter visits.

Checklist for residential/overnight trips and tours

A Pre-planning checks

1. Has permission been received *in writing* from the head on behalf of the governing body for a trip to go ahead?

2. Is there an agreed Teacher IC (Teacher In Charge)?

3. Has the destination been approved and visited? (A destination that is being used for the first time should be visited — most tour operators now organise free risk assessment visits for party leaders. No matter how good the tour rep, there is no substitute for a personal risk assessment.)

4. Is the tour company well known and recommended? If not, can it produce *written* references from other schools?

5. Is the tour company you intend to use ABTA or ATOL bonded?

6. If organising the trip in-house you should be able to provide assurances about destinations, accommodation and activities in the same way that you would expect a commercial operator to.

7. Has a letter to parents been produced and checked (this should include destination details, dates, brief rationale, cost per pupil and a return booking slip)?

B Health, safety and security

1. Has the tour company provided a **risk assessment** *in writing* of the destination and activities?

2. Has a **school in-house risk assessment** been carried out and lodged with the school office?

→

Checklist for residential/overnight trips and tours continued

3. Is the party leader and their staff suitably skilled and/or qualified to take the trip?

4. Has the party leader or any other member of staff attended any relevant training in order to lead the intended trip?

5. Does the school insurance cover pupils and staff for the intended activities?

6. Are staff aware of any specific hazards that may be encountered on the trip?

7. Do any of the travelling staff hold first aid qualifications or recent training/experience?

8. For Europe – have E111/European health insurance cards been acquired?

9. Does everyone who needs one have a passport and/or visa, or are you using a group passport?

10. Have you completed a List of Travellers (LOT) form?

11. For non-EU countries – is medical insurance cover included in the cost of the trip?

12. Have you organised an emergency school contact?

13. Are you aware of the school critical incident plan (CIP) for dealing with very serious injuries/illness?

14. How will you deal with minor injuries/illness?

15. Will medical detail and consent forms be completed for each child?

16. What procedures are there for accounting for pupils in the event of an evacuation from a building?

C Planning the trip – details

1. Has the tour company provided a risk assessment and a named UK contact?

2. Has a list of staff been agreed?

3. Is there a final list of pupil names?

4. What is the exact cost per pupil (provide a breakdown)?

5. How will the trip be paid for and what method will you use to collect money?

6. What are the deadlines for payment?

7. What are the arrangements for transport?

8. Kit and equipment (hire or buy) – has a list been issued to parents?

Checklist for residential/overnight trips and tours continued

9. Has a full itinerary been agreed and published prior to the trip?

10. Have contact details for resort/hotel manager, party leader, second IC and accommodation been sent to parents and the school office?

11. Has a parent briefing evening been arranged?

D During the trip

1. Has a behaviour code been issued to each member of the party?

2. Has a duty rota been arranged for staff and senior pupils?

3. What rewards and sanctions will you use while away from school?

4. How will pupils be routinely supervised?

5 What procedures for roll calling will you use?

6. Is a trip bank to be in operation?

7. How will you deal with behavioural and emotional problems?

8. Where is the nearest hospital to your destination?

9. Will you have access to a resort manager/rep or a guide who speaks the local language?

10. How will you safeguard important documents and data (passports, medical data, etc.)?

Being able to answer all of the above questions will ensure that you've thought about the trip in detail and planned for most reasonable eventualities. The work involved in answering these questions means that you'll want some help at the planning and organisation stage.

Why not try this?

Try using checklists with the pupils to help them organise themselves and record details about the trip.

Planning the core learning activities

The practical, physical, intellectual, emotional or social learning activities that your pupils will be involved in will most likely form the prime motivation for running your trip. But don't forget that teacher learning can take place side by side with pupil learning.

However, there is quite a lot of research evidence that suggests we don't even take full advantage of the opportunities for pupil learning while on field trips. The following problems are most often highlighted in the findings.

- Teachers may not prepare their pupils sufficiently for the trip they are about to take.
- Teachers may not research the destination or learning activities for their trip in sufficient detail.
- Teachers may not allow time for follow-up work after a trip.
- Teachers use a pedagogic approach that is more suited to classroom teaching.
- Teachers may not be aware of their roles on field trips when venue staff are also involved (e.g. a museum workshop or guided tour).

These problems can be caused or exacerbated by: a lack of experience; school organisational conditions that produce barriers, such as a lack of time to prepare or follow up; the prevalence of examinations cutting into teaching time; and difficulties for teachers in organising preliminary visits to trip venues and destinations.

It is also noted in the research that some teachers appear to want learning to happen through osmosis. James Kisiel (2005) calls this an 'exposure motivation', where teachers just want children to be exposed to a phenomenon or environment that they otherwise wouldn't experience. Absolutely nothing wrong with that, and these sorts of experiences are also very common on cultural tours, ski trips, sports tours, student exchanges and expeditions. However, in the midst of our current performance driven education culture, exposure is harder to justify to your senior management – it suggests a lack of focus. Far easier to justify and more likely to help achieve specific learning targets are trips that have a curriculum connection which directly affects pupils' understanding of a particular topic. If this is your aim, the following dos and don'ts are worth considering.

Do:

- Use something like a 'three-part unit' plan: preparation learning–trip activity learning–follow-up learning (see below).
- Use a trip to contextualise previous learning with real-life examples.
- Use a trip to prepare for a new topic.
- Plan your trip to focus on a key aspect of your current syllabus.
- Have a plan B and be able to react to things going wrong or to changeable conditions.
- Talk to venue staff if they are going to be part of your learning activity or presentation (see 'The risk assessment, Visiting the site of your trip' on p47).

- Keep passive learning to a minimum – pupils can get a good deal of this at school; the trip is a time for them to be actively involved in their own learning.
- Allow time for pupils' reflection about the visit and connection to the wider world around them (see Figure 2.4, Kolb's learning cycle, on page 34).

Don't:

- Try to achieve too much in one trip – focus on one or two aspects at a time that can really help.
- Expect too much of venue staff or guides. Education officers in museums and field centres often design their activities for a very broad audience as school parties vary so much. You can't expect them to do it all for you.
- Design lengthy independent learning activities – give fixed deadlines for each activity and make them short.
- Treat the school trip as a one-off day out – integrate it into your teaching and learning objectives for the term/year.

Learning models

A 'three-part unit' plan was suggested by much of the early literature on school trips when research into this area of learning began to grow in the 1990s. It seems intuitive now, but then it was a rarely followed model of learning on school trips. A classic three-part unit of study might look like this:

- Preliminary preparation for the trip – preparing pupils for what they are about to experience.
- Learning activities on the trip – building on preliminary work.
- Follow-up work – reflection on learning or connecting to the wider field of knowledge.

By encouraging follow-up work, the three-part unit model provides integrity to the learning experience and introduces an element of reflection on learning beyond the trip experience. It also encourages pupils to position their learning within the world more generally. This method of learning has similarities to Kolb's learning cycle (see Figure 2.4), where reflection, generalisation and testing follow any experience to provide sustainable learning.

Exponents of assessment for learning (AfL) will recognise reflection as a key component of that practice/philosophy, and understand its effectiveness in encouraging self-awareness in pupils' learning.

By presenting your trip with some sort of theoretical underpinnings to support it, you make it easier for senior managers, colleagues, parents and pupils to see its value.

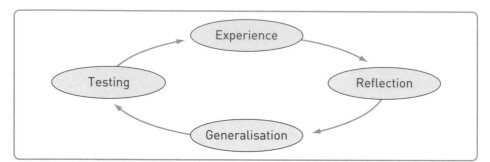

Fig. 2.4 Kolb's learning cycle (1984)

Using commercial educational trip and tour operators

Many of these companies are excellent and work hard to provide you with a good service. Others are best avoided. While good educational travel firms should belong to ABTA (Association of British Travel Agents) or ATOL (Air Travel Organisers' Licensing) before you even think of using them, membership of these organisations is not a guarantee of the quality of their service specific to school groups. Consider the following tips.

- Ask for an inspection visit as part of the package. If the tour company can't offer one, they should at least offer you a thorough activity specific risk assessment for the actual destination. If they can't do that, walk away.
- Ask for contact details of previously satisfied clients from other schools. Insist on at least three different contacts up and down the country. Telephone them, rather than emailing, as a phone call can be more revealing.
- If they are a new company, ask where the staff are from and if they've worked in the industry before.
- Ask about their training for guides, resort reps and instructors that you might use.
- Ask to see a copy of the client list.
- Never book the cheapest firm unless you are sure they are going to be able to offer what you want.
- Don't pay a deposit until you are happy with the arrangements – study the contract carefully.
- Be sure of the refund policy and terms and conditions of booking.
- If you are staying overnight, you must insist on seeing up-to-date details of the hotel/hostel and its location and facilities. If you're not happy, walk away. Never accept a last-minute change.
- Get anything that has been agreed verbally in black and white too.

- Always keep emails and letters and take the name of anyone you speak to by phone.
- If you find a good travel firm, share the information. Post a thread on the TES school trips website forum and let people know about it (www.tes.co.uk/forums).
- Establish a relationship with a good travel firm and do your best to maintain it. People work harder for you when they can put a face to a name and know you are someone to be respected.

Outdoor pursuits centres

A quick glance at the Institute for Outdoor Learning's website (www.outdoor-learning.org) reveals a host of centres that provide all manner of outdoor pursuits and activities specifically catering for children, families and young adults.

Most are excellent, but accommodation, facilities, expertise and qualification levels vary from place to place. Most will be members of the Institute for Outdoor Learning (IOL) and/or the Adventure Activities Licensing Authority (AALA) (www.aala.org.uk). Membership of these organisations should give you some assurance that they are well run and inspected regularly. However, membership doesn't automatically mean that these centres will provide what you want for your pupils. The only way to know that is to make a visit yourself and seek referrals from other satisfied teachers.

The feature that attracts schools to adventure and outdoor pursuits centres in the first place is that they offer expert instructors who are capable of being responsible for the safety of the children in their care. However, you still have a duty to select a safe and reputable centre with instructors who are properly qualified for the activities they are running. So, find out what activities they run, who the governing bodies are and what qualifications the instructors should have: do your homework.

Why not try this?

As well as ATOL, ABTA, AALA and IOL membership, look for membership of the School Travel Forum (STF) and the Quality Badge awarded by the Council for Learning Outside the Classroom (www.lotcqualitybadge.org.uk).

Money and funding

Getting the financial side of school trips right is of utmost importance. As with many other aspects of your job, your school may have a policy concerning the financial management of trips. If it doesn't, get some colleagues together, write one and present it to the head teacher – take the lead!

> **Beware!**
>
> If you knowingly mismanage a trip budget or mislead whoever is paying for it, you could face criminal charges if the details come to light. The only way forward is to be completely transparent about what happens to any money that changes hands. Some schools won't let teaching staff handle money at all, and despite this being inconvenient on some occasions it is a more professional way to operate. In business, sales teams rarely handle the cash; that's down to the accounts department. When you are planning a trip, you're effectively the salesperson who needs to sell an idea to senior management or the EVC, and then the product to the consumer (the pupils and parents or a funding body).

Here are ten general guidelines to follow. It doesn't matter if the money comes from a funding body like a local authority, a charitable trust or individuals such as parents or even pupils themselves.

1. **Budget**. Be very clear about how much money you need for your trip and how and where it will be spent – write this down as a statement when proposing the trip to your head or EVC.

2. **Try not to handle cash**. If you have to, make sure you record what you have been given *as soon as you get it* – keep a dedicated notebook for such purposes.

3. **Never take trip payment money home** with you: cash or cheques.

4. **Never use your own bank account** or set one up in your name for trip funds.

5. **Use your school bursar or finance officer** to receive and record payments and bank all money.

6. **Keep your own immaculate records** – spreadsheets are a must. You should check your records with your school finance officer at regular intervals during the payment period.

7. **Provide documentary evidence for all spending** or cash advances (receipts and invoices). If your finance officer is doing the spending for you prior to the trip, ask for copies for your file.

8. **Never take money from pupils during a trip**. You may want to set up a pocket money bank for the kids to draw on while away, particularly if they are young and getting used to money. Factor this into the total cost of the trip for each pupil and collect it before you go away. Make cash available at different stages of the day.

9. **Share information with colleagues**. Get someone else to check over your figures before you go and agree your spending records while you're on your trip.

10. **Write a spending report**. Justify your spending to your finance officer at the end of your trip. It doesn't need to be a long document. Do this in conjunction with your documentary evidence (see point 7 above).

Did you know...?

In maintained schools you can't charge for the full cost of a trip if it takes place inside normal school hours or is part of a syllabus towards an examination, part of the national curriculum or part of statutory religious education.

You can ask parents for a voluntary contribution.

You can charge for trips such as adventure holidays, ski trips, expeditions and weekend trips as they are optional extras.

Adding extra charges and contingency funds

On some school trips, particularly longer residential ones, it has become common practice to add extra charges to the cost of the trip. This tends to happen when a commercial travel firm is involved and sets a price for the trip. The travel firm's customer is 'the school' rather than the pupils or parents and so in this way the school acts as an agent between the pupils/parents and the travel firm. Commercial travel agents take commission in such circumstances – it's how they make their money. Schools don't take commission but do often add a figure on to the cost of a trip per person, although they don't always make it clear why. In the example below, two common 'extras' have been added on, but a third 'other' charge is also included.

Hockey tour to Holland (per person cost breakdown)	
Cost of a weekend hockey tour to Holland per person – includes flights, bed and breakfast accommodation, transfers to and from airport, packed lunches and evening meals. With 'School Sports Travel Company'	£150
School add-on cost of tour kit per person (T-shirts, etc.)	£25
School add-on cost of cinema tickets for one evening's entertainment	£5
'Other' costs	*£20*
Total cost of trip per pupil	**£200**

What is the 'other' costs charge of £20 for?

A surprising number of trips use this charge but rarely explain it to their customers (pupils and parents), and it is often hidden in an overall charge for 'kit and evening entertainment' which, in the case above, would amount to £50 even though the kit and entertainment comes to just £30; the extra £20 is lost in the total cost. The charge is not necessarily a bad thing or done dishonestly, but it should be open to scrutiny, recorded in 'the books' and listed in the letter to parents.

A contingency charge is often levied in order to create an emergency fund, from which things like taxis to hospital can be paid for or the cost of medicines or ambulance rides can be met. Tour trophies, awards and prizes for the best room can be bought from such funds, as can presents for hard-working coaches, instructors or bus drivers.

Be prepared!

Why use cash for emergencies – can't you rely on travel insurance to sort your problems out for you?

All good in theory and on TV adverts, but it never works like that in practice. You're likely to need to pay for emergency items/services in the middle of the night, and in some countries ambulance drivers will happily give you a bill while you're sat in the hospital waiting room and expect payment there and then.

As a teacher in charge of a tour or trip, you should never use your own money to pay for anything other than what you need or use for yourself. Having a tour contingency/emergency fund with equal contributions from each paying pupil allows you a sense of ease, knowing you have funds available to deal with emergencies should they arise. It's a kind of insurance scheme in its simplest form. You also have money available to reward those pupils who have made a conspicuous contribution to everyone's enjoyment, or just to buy each of them a souvenir of their stay.

Parents are unlikely to be reluctant to contribute if they know what it is for and how it will be used. But you must justify its use and calculate the amount carefully. Rarely is it justifiable on a day trip unless this involves travel to another country, where if a child fell seriously ill a member of staff might need to remain behind and so find accommodation. You can always give the money back if you choose not to use it, but make everything crystal clear.

Did you know…?

Parents need to give their express permission for their children to be involved in any type of trip away from school. For trips that involve a charge they need to agree formally to pay the amount stated on a formal letter.

What should a budget look like?

Budgets take many forms and unless you've been trained in bookkeeping you may be unsure of what to produce. With a trip budget you really only need to know a few things.

1. **What is the total cost of the trip with everything taken into account?** Including entry costs; travel; accommodation; food; extra costs you might be adding for kit, trip awards, or contingency funds, etc.; activity instruction costs; and insurance.

2. **How many children and staff are you taking?** With commercially provided trips you'll often be offered free staff places on a 1:10 staff/pupil ratio. So if you want to take more staff, you'll need to budget for the extra cost.

3. **Where is the money coming from?** School or LA, voluntary contributions, or are you charging parents?

4. **What is the exact breakdown of costs?** As far as possible try to predict exactly what the money will be spent on. Ticket prices and transport costs are normally fixed, so that's easy. But if you want to travel by public transport in France, for example, and you don't know the exact cost until you get to the bus station, you'll need to provide a rough idea of the cash you'll need for this activity.

5. **How will the money be spent?** Will the school be paying a firm or firms by cheque, electronic transfer or cash? How will contingency fund money be spent and by whom?

6. **How much do I charge per pupil?** This depends on the type of trip. If you are only charging entry fees and transport, the answer is simple – just divide the total cost by the number of pupils.

7. **Are there any extra costs to plan for?** Even all-inclusive deals are not all inclusive. Experience dealing with travel firms suggests that what you see is not always what you get. Will pupils need lockers at the end of a day's activity? Will drinks be provided as part of the all-inclusive lunch or will they be added on? Have all the evening activities actually been paid for? What if your party gets charged for excess baggage?

8. **Do I need a contingency travel fund?** Yes! Even if you are travelling a matter of yards away from school, it's important to have access to some cash. Not your own if possible (keep all receipts if you ever do use your own). Even a £10 contingency fund can get you out of trouble if you need to take a taxi to hospital, or buy a bottle of water or sunscreen on a hot day at the zoo.

9. **What is the plan if a pupil drops out of the trip?** Ensure that the terms and conditions for booking allow you some freedom. If you can find a replacement then your problems are solved, but you don't want to be left with a place on a

trip that has to be paid for and nobody to pay for it. Make any booking terms and conditions clear to parents. They could be asked to book directly with the travel firm, that way their contract is with the service provider and you are not involved. If a pupil drops out of a day trip, you are less likely to have such big financial worries. But if they drop out on the actual day of the trip, someone will have to arrange for that child to be supervised at school or sent home.

Figure 2.5 is an example of a simple Excel spreadsheet budget for a ski trip. Note that in this case, money is paid to the school, and the school then pays the travel company. It's just as easy to pay direct, but extras like trip hoodies and awards might need to be paid for separately.

Senior School Ski Trip Budget 2010

	Ski Trip Fund	Price	No. of pupils	Totals
A	Cost per pupil (payable to school)	825	50	41250
B	Cost per pupil (payable to 'School Ski World')	775	50	*38750*
C	Drop-out deposits retained (£80 pp)	80		0
	Number of 'free place' staff		5	
	Staff ski hire voluntary contribution pp			0
D	*Difference between A and B (contingency fund)*			*2500*

Note
A is cost per pupil with cost of tour hoodie, night skiing, swimming, contingency, certificates and prize fund added
B is cost as per 'School Ski World' invoice which includes free staff places on a 1:10 ratio

Other costs paid from difference contingency (D)

		Price	No. of pupils	Totals
E	Hooded tops	24	55	1320
F	Radio (2 pack)	75	1	75
G	Emergency first aid kit	50	1	50
				0
H	**Expected spending (costs to be finalised in resort):**			0
	Night skiing & swimming			0
	Certificates			0
	Prizes			0

Note
Remaining contingency fund travels with party
This fund provides emergency cash to cover costs such as ambulances, medication, and other transport or replacement costs prior to an insurance claim.

		Price	No. of pupils	Totals
I	*Remaining contingency*			*1055*
J	Surplus from previous trips carried forward			900
	Contingency + surplus (I+J)			1955
K	Extra adults/staff paying for selves (e.g. spouses of staff)	775	2	1550

L	**Total to be paid to 'School Ski World'** Totals of B+H+K			**40300**

Fig 2.5: Excel spreadsheet budget for a ski trip

Grants and help for low income families

Think carefully about the possibility of getting a grant for a trip before you really get down to planning it. LAs and other government organisations may have incentive funds for particular activities of an educational nature, so have a good look around. If you don't ask, you don't get!

The socioeconomic status of your pupils must be taken into account when you plan a trip. Many parents find it increasingly difficult to fund school trips, so if you have pupils with parents in the low income bracket, grants may be a good place to start. And while free trips are best, you needn't restrict your pupils' horizons to local trips: it is possible to travel further afield on smaller budgets, either through travel bursaries or commercial sponsorship. Under certain circumstances low income families won't have to pay costs for a residential trip if they meet certain criteria. At the time of writing the government's guidelines are as follows:

'Schools can charge for the cost of accommodation during overnight school trips, but the school may not charge more than the accommodation actually costs.

Where the visit takes place wholly or mainly during school hours, pupils whose parents get the following benefits aren't required to pay any charge:

- *Income Support*
- *Income Based Job Seekers Allowance*
- *Support under part VI of the Immigration and Asylum Act 1999*
- *Child Tax Credit provided the parent is not entitled to Working Tax Credit and their annual income does not exceed £16,040*
- *Guaranteed State Pension Credit*

This is in addition to having a free school lunch entitlement.

A similar entitlement applies when:

- *the visit takes place outside of school hours but it is a necessary part of the National Curriculum*
- *the visit forms part of the syllabus for an examination that the school is preparing the pupil to sit*
- *the visit is part of religious education.'*

(www.direct.gov.uk/en/Parents/Schoolslearninganddevelopment/SchoolLife)

Local charitable trusts can also support children from low income families to take advantage of residential trips and other educational ventures by paying all or part of the costs depending on ability to pay.

Fundraising and sponsorship

If the full amount needed for a trip is not available for each pupil in the form of ready cash, you might also want to consider fundraising. The same ten general guidelines for dealing with money apply though.

Some schools rent out their car parks for 'car boot sales' or charge shoppers a flat daily fee for parking if they are close to local shops. Proceeds from school fetes can contribute to trips, as can those from car washing mornings or sponsored walks – the possibilities are endless. Don't be afraid to contact local businesses for sponsorship for trips either. A hundred pounds is a huge amount for many families but a tiny amount for big business, so take your chances and ask around. By seeking sponsorship from local businesses you can set up a fund to help low income parents pay for trips for their children. How this is managed is then up to the school, but it's worth a try, especially if most parents at your school fall into the low income bracket. Even a small donation to a class trip, say £50, can significantly reduce the cost per pupil.

Spending money on a trip

If you want to take cash with you from your contingency fund you'll need to take some precautions against theft. You'll also need to be able to account for every penny you spend. Here are some suggestions:

- Divide the cash up among your staff, recording who has what. This way, if one staff member loses the money or has it stolen, your losses are minimised.
- Use sealable sandwich bags in which to keep cash and receipts for your contingency fund. Get the other staff to do the same.
- Keep every receipt and ask for one if not offered at point of sale. Record everything in your trip log or a pocket-sized notebook.
- At the end of the day, make sure your spending tallies with what you've got left and each staff member still has the amount of cash you expected.
- Don't spend all the money at once – budget for the day, week or however long you're away.
- Only spend money on justifiable items.

Spending money abroad?

If you're going abroad and taking a contingency/emergency cash fund, make sure that the amount of cash you're taking can be covered by your insurance. Also try to start with the currency you need before you leave school. Get your finance officer or bursar to withdraw the currency for you and return any unspent money in the same currency. Don't be tempted to convert it back to your home currency yourself.

Passports, visas and health

Trying to get a student into a country without a visa is one of the most difficult things I've ever done. It was my fault, I suppose – we shouldn't have taken her parents' word for it that she had a visa for our destination. A two-hour-long negotiation with stern-faced, armed immigration officials was not something we could have planned for.

Nevertheless, we got through it after many phone calls and our student was allowed entry with restrictions concerning her stay. I have to confess that it was a little galling as we'd made a big deal about visas, knowing how many overseas students we had and that entry requirements for non-EU passengers travelling within the EU were pretty strict. No excuses, we got it wrong that time. Here are some tips to help you avoid the same situation:

- Travel with passports that are in date with plenty of time to run before they expire. Don't travel with a passport that will expire while you're away.
- Visas need to be applied for when travelling to some destinations. If in doubt contact the Foreign and Commonwealth Office via its website (www.fco.gov.uk), or the embassy for your destination country.
- European health insurance cards (the new E111 form) should be up to date for every passenger. Visit www.e111.org.uk/apply.html to get a new one.
- If you're travelling outside the EU, make sure that your travel insurance provides adequate health cover for your party and covers the activities you'll be doing.
- Allow time to get any immunisations organised. Don't forget that parents need to give consent for children to be immunised. See the Foreign and Commonwealth Office website for details (www.fco.gov.uk).

TOP TIP!

Although it is illegal to copy (or forge) a passport, it's a good idea to travel with a photocopy of each person's passport, visa and health insurance details in case the originals get lost.

Travelling in the EU with non-EU pupils? – visas or a List of Travellers form?

The British Council issues the List of Travellers (LOT) form in the UK, for school trips to countries in the EU for pupils on the trip who are of a non-EU nationality. (This won't cover non-EU adult staff.) The form allows the pupils to go on the trip without getting individual visas. It is occasionally referred to as a 'visa waiver form'. If all the pupils on the trip are from the UK or EU countries then the form isn't needed. The forms are officially accepted by the following states: Austria,

Belgium, Cyprus, Czech Republic, Denmark, Finland, France, Germany, Greece, Hungary, Ireland, Italy, Latvia, Luxembourg, Poland, Portugal, Spain, Sweden, the Netherlands, Romania, as well as Iceland, Norway and Switzerland (see www.britishcouncil.org/home-information-centre-list-of-travellers-scheme.htm). An application will take up to six weeks and the group must travel with a named group leader who is over 21 years of age and who holds a full British passport (see www.direct.gov.uk/en/TravelAndTransport/Passports for more details).

Insurance

This is an absolute must. Some schools' insurance policies include cover for children away from school on educational trips and may also include insurance for some adventurous sports. Travel firms will also include appropriate insurance for the activities they provide, but they will charge you for it, which is a waste if your pupils are already covered. Travel insurance offers peace of mind when travelling short distances too; you don't have to go on a world tour to need this type of insurance. Even a trip to the nearest zoo can benefit from good insurance cover if a child falls ill with E.-coli or has personal belongings stolen.

Here's what to do:

● Check the details of your school's insurance cover – what does it include and what doesn't it include? Is the insured amount sufficient for your chosen activity? Your EVC or school bursar should have this information to hand.

● If you are using a travel firm find out what level of cover their insurance can offer. If you don't need it, don't use it (and don't pay for it), but do double- and triple-check this to be safe.

● Make sure that you have access to the insurance details while you are travelling – in your day bag or briefcase, whatever you travel with.

● Communicate your insurance status to your pupils' parents when they book the trip with you. Make sure that they understand the nature of the trip and what is insured on it, especially if it is part of the overall cost. It makes sense to communicate this for your sake too – should anything go wrong, you can be sure you've covered all bases.

Whatever you do, though, don't forget that insurance is not protection against something going wrong; it is a method of dealing with the aftermath of an event, injury or loss. To prevent something from going wrong, you either have to stay at home for ever, or have to try to control the risks to an extent that allows you to carry on with life. The risk assessment is what this is all about and is the keystone of planning a school trip.

The risk assessment

Risk assessments are a big part of our lives: they've taken over nearly every activity we are involved in. You hear apocryphal stories all the time about children having to wear goggles to put up Christmas decorations in school halls, or 'Health and Safety' banning the use of simple items like stepladders unless you've had training. On the one hand, an awareness of risk and methods of controlling risks is an excellent and very helpful tool in our teaching toolkit. On the other hand, it's a nuisance, made worse by people who don't really understand the concepts of risk assessment and health and safety and who apply inappropriate measures without any real thought. The last thing that teachers want to do is restrict the freedom of children to learn and grow.

Is there a better way of thinking about the risk assessment?

There has to be! At the moment, many of us view the risk assessment as a necessary evil, a bolt-on legal requirement. Chapter 1 briefly referred to risk assessments and suggested that there was a way that we could integrate them with CPD and preparations for school inspections. I'd like to try to reframe the way we think about the risk assessment as a component of teachers' reflective CPD activities.

Being a reflective practitioner means different things to different people, of course, but to many it suggests having an awareness of your own practice and the need to adapt and improve it. Reflective practice is best when it involves others in the process and responds to their needs, be they pupils or colleagues.

A risk assessment is surely a tool for reflection on a particular activity. If we consider a risk assessment alongside a simple reflective practice process, it's possible to see the similarities between the two activities (see the table overleaf).

Both processes follow a reflective evaluative pattern and can go on indefinitely in a circular manner as an activity evolves. Indeed, both processes can also fall into three categories that are commonly used to organise risk assessments:

Generic

A generic risk assessment is likely to apply to a particular activity wherever it takes place. In the same way, reflection on practice such as dealing with behaviour can probably occur in, and relate to, a broad range of contexts.

Specific

The context and location of an activity mean that risks are specific and need to be considered accordingly. In the same way, reflection on practice in a science lab will have differing outcomes to a PE lesson.

Simple risk assessment process	Simple reflective practice process
Identify hazard	Identify area of practice for scrutiny
What are the risks, who do they affect and how likely are they?	What elements of teaching/learning might be improved?
What are the existing control measures?	What is wrong with the current method?
What additional control measures might be needed?	What changes could be made to improve teaching/learning?

Ongoing

Where conditions (such as weather, personnel, location, availability of an activity or illness of staff) may change so too do the associated risks, and so an ongoing reaction to risk is required. In classroom practice we do the same when we need to adapt a lesson plan due to a large number of absentees, illness, disruption, or because we've worked out a better way of teaching a particular element of a topic and reacted to the needs of the children.

The suggestion that we should try to integrate the process of assessing risk with our reflective practice might go some way to reducing the burden. By actually using the risk assessment to inform cogent consideration of our practice when on school trips, we are using it as a method of reflective professional development, where we are enhancing the likelihood of success for any given activity. Furthermore, it's a useful exercise to carry out with newly qualified teachers on their first school trip, as it's an opportunity for conversation and reflection about practice where ideas for risk control measures can be shared.

Nevertheless, part of the frustration with the whole area of health and safety and risk assessment is the amount of extra paperwork needed to carry out a relatively simple task. A quick glance at the Teachernet website, which rather pessimistically stores all of its planning resources in its 'emergency' section (www.teachernet. gov.uk/emergencies/resources), provides a bewildering array of forms and checklists to complete before the trip takes place.

Forward thinking schools are now starting to integrate planning forms, checklists and risk assessments into their computer based management information systems (MIS), where pupil data is easily accessed. This is a fantastic step forward for managing all the information you'll need to acquire before you go on a trip, but you'll still have to work through the reflective process of considering risks the old-fashioned way – using the old grey matter and talking things through with colleagues. What I'm suggesting here is that risk assessment be part of the planning process right from the start and be integrated into our collaborative discussions about the aims and objectives of the trip. What helps with this process is the site risk assessment visit.

Visiting the site of your trip

Having discussed the ideas for the trip in a meeting with colleagues you will want to get more information about the location and what's on offer. If it is within your budget a site visit is an excellent way of answering a whole range of questions in one go. If you're planning a curriculum based trip a site visit is the only way of knowing that you won't be wasting your time. Educational travel is big business so many companies offer inspection trips as part of the package if you book with them.

Advantages of an Inspection visit

- Knowing the lay of the land and how to move around the site is a huge benefit. You'll be able to see the location of exits, first aid points and areas for lunch and shelter.

- You'll know how long it takes to get there and where to park and meet coaches, where there are safe places to cross roads and what the neighbourhood is like.

- You'll meet the people who'll be helping you – museum guides, rangers, wardens, instructors. You'll be able to assess their personalities and talk to them about your trip and your pupils. Make arrangements to meet before you set out to avoid disappointment.

- Meeting the people will help you to finalise the plan for your trip, maybe sort out last-minute changes to the itinerary or adapt a worksheet to take advantage of a new exhibit.

Top tips:

- Plan your learning activities around the facilities, don't try to do it the other way round.

- Listen to the advice of people who know.

- Work out where the nearest A&E hospital is in relation to your destination.

- A visit will help you to know your alternative travel routes – buses, tubes and trains, etc.

And specifically for residential and overseas trips:

- Check out all the promised facilities in the brochure.

- Check the details that your travel firm have provided. →

Advantages of an inspection visit continued

- Be aware of the local amenities and the safety of the general area.
- Assess the safety of the accommodation and its fire escape routes.
- Meet instructors, check equipment and get assurances on quality and qualifications – don't rely on someone else's say-so.
- Get answers to all your questions and insist on detail.
- Never accept anything that will be 'finalised when you arrive'. Inevitably it'll be forgotten until you arrive, and then bodged.
- Be aware of special treatment on the site visit or inspection tour. If it doesn't feel genuine, your party could get short shrift when you arrive.
- Check the quality of the rooms that your pupils will be staying in. If it's not good enough for you, it's not good enough for them. Squeezing four teenagers into a room designed for two adults is a cynical old trick. Don't accept it unless proper beds and facilities are provided.
- Take photographs of important aspects of the trip – accommodation, dining facilities, equipment, transport options, venues for activities and anything else that can add detail to your team briefings or presentations to parents.
- Never sign an agreement with a travel firm or hand over any money for the main trip before a satisfactory site visit has been carried out or you are sure that what you see in a brochure is what you'll get.
- If you can't get to the site, insist on independent references from teachers who've been satisfied in the past.

And the golden rule for any site visit is that if you see something you're not happy with and it can't be fixed, just walk away – you're going to be responsible for someone else's children and you need to be confident.

Communication and information

At an early stage it's important to sort out what information is needed. This will entail a whole range of communication methods, including meetings and briefings, management information systems, letters and emails.

You need to take meetings seriously right from the start. In the current climate, where the threat of litigation is ever present, a detailed and appropriate paper trail needs to exist to justify the decisions you make. You'll need to be organised and notes or minutes should be filed appropriately. There isn't a need to write up and distribute formal minutes for every meeting, but you do need to record agreement in some way, perhaps by asking those present to sign the handwritten notes if they agree with them (read them back to them during a plenary). Even meetings held during trips can be of importance, so a notebook is an essential requirement for a party leader on a school trip. Changing plans on a trip? Record them in black and white.

The planning meeting

The first meeting will be your planning meeting, where you set the tone for the trip and invite contributions from colleagues. This may form part of a department or key stage meeting where the colleagues who are likely to join you are already present. If it is not a curriculum based venture then you'll have the problem of bringing your team together in one place for half an hour – a not inconsiderable challenge in itself In a busy school. Here's a suggestion for your planning agenda:

1. Where, why, how, when and who?
2. What are the learning aims and objectives?
3. How will the trip enhance learning?
4. What work will pupils do before, during and after the trip?
5. Discussion around the planning checklist (see page 29) – distribute leadership responsibilities.
6. What will it cost and where will the money come from?
7. What information do we need from parents?
8. Is any specialist help needed to cater for special pupil needs?
9. Risk assessment considerations.

Make sure that your meetings result in action and set deadlines for completion. Never leave a meeting without agreeing the next step that you all need to take.

The letter to parents

Once you've had a planning meeting, gone through the checklist and received permission from your head or EVC, you can write to parents about the trip. You should try to make your trip sound as exciting and useful as possible, of course, but also provide key information that is easy to access. Here are two examples, one for a day trip and the other introducing a week-long overseas trip.

Example

30th September 2009

Dear Parents

Design & Technology A-level seminar – Institute of Education, University of London
Monday 7th December 2009
The Design & Technology department will be leading a trip to this extremely useful seminar for lower sixth form design students.

The seminar will focus on design strategies for major projects and will include a number of high-profile speakers from industry and leading design consultancies. This is a rare opportunity to hear from so many highly skilled and talented designers gathered in one place. The pupils will get an excellent sense of what real designers do and how they think and work.

We will leave from Trumpton railway station at 8.30am, travelling by train and tube to Russell Square in central London for the start of the seminar at 10.45am. A packed lunch will be available in the student union café. You will not be charged for the trip as it falls mostly in the normal school day, but you might like to make a voluntary contribution of £10 towards travel costs. We will aim to return to school for approximately 6pm.

I would be grateful if you could complete and return the consent slip below. I look forward to your son/daughter joining us on this exciting and interesting trip.

Yours sincerely
John Smith
e-mail: john.smith@designtrip.co.uk

Dear Mr Smith

I give my son/daughter.. permission to attend the D&T trip to the Institute of Education on 7th December 2009. I *can/cannot* enclose a voluntary contribution for £10 (cheque made payable to the school and sent to the address above).

Yours sincerely

Name............................ Signature.....................Date.........

This letter provides the basic details and allows for a simple consent form to be completed, which also confirms whether the parents can or cannot pay a voluntary contribution. The letter is written in good English, has a simple structure that is easy to follow and contains a central paragraph with all the main details in it. Of course, you could put the details into bullet points or put key details in bold.

Why not try this?

How about providing a second copy of your letter in another commonly spoken language in your area? This will help to ensure you include as many of your pupils and their parents as possible.

Example

Dear Parents

28th September 2009

Ski Trip 2010 – Austria
In 2010 we will be returning, by popular demand, to Schladming during the Easter holiday period. We will depart on 27th March and return on 3rd April. This trip is an excellent opportunity for skiers of all levels, but especially for beginners.

The trip is run on a very successful format that combines excellent care of the pupils with world-class instruction, fantastic scenery and great value for money. If you would like to book a place for your son/daughter please complete the form below and send it to me at the school address no later than 16th October. The **fully inclusive** cost will be £825.00.

Further information, including flight details and itinerary, will follow and a parent briefing evening will be held later in the term. I will also send a confirmation letter to you following receipt of the £80 deposit which will be used to book your son/daughter's flight. Please do get in touch, via email in the first instance, if I can answer any questions before you book.

Yours sincerely

Jane Smith
Teacher IC Skiing
e-mail: jane.smith@schoolskitrip.co.uk

→

Ski Trip Booking Form
Dear Miss Smith

I would like my son(s)/daughter(s):

.... *(Name(s) as in passport)*
to join the Trumpton Community College ski trip at Easter in 2010.

I enclose an £80 non-refundable deposit and understand that I am requesting a
flight to be booked on an airline in my son/daughter's name by 'Ski Trumpton',
and that I will be asked to provide the balance of £745 in due course.

Yours sincerely

Print............................Sign...................Date...........
(Name of parent/guardian)

Your email...

Because the second trip is a little more complicated the letter is more vague, but it still provides the essential details. In this case the deposit is non-refundable as scheduled 'low cost' flights can only be booked once names and numbers are known. If a pupil were to pull out of the trip, a 'name change charge' would apply, or the cost of the ticket would still have to be met.

Note that the letter promises a briefing meeting and further details. If you promise something, you must deliver and do so in good time.

Briefing meetings

Sometimes called presentation evenings, these are vital for trips that include adventurous activities or extreme sports where there are important issues surrounding insurance and safety that parents who are new to the activity will want to know.

Presentation evenings are often held at the start of a term. Teachers invite parents along prior to taking bookings, in order to sell the trip. They are a great way to get numbers up on your trip, but require parents to attend in the first place. Another way to do this is to advertise your trip in a termly mail-out or newsletter and take bookings by return, then invite those who have booked to come along for a briefing.

Whichever system you use, the important thing is that you get to meet the parents of the children you are taking away. This is great for you but even better for the parents as they can put a face to a name and learn about your approach and leadership style, which is very reassuring for mums and dads.

During the briefing, parents will want to know the basics such as timings and places, but they'll also appreciate a flavour of what the trip will be like. Think about the following suggestions for good practice during a briefing:

- Use appropriate technology such as PowerPoint, but whatever you do don't read it word for word!
- Give information handouts.
- Use photos and video to provide a flavour of the activities and places.
- Invite a pupil along who has attended the trip before, to talk about their experiences.
- Give an example of a typical day.
- If it's the first time for this trip, invite a travel firm rep to come along to help flesh out the details.
- If you are running the trip independently, use your inspection/risk assessment trip photos to help explain things.
- Show the risk assessment on your slide show.
- Talk about the school's drinking, smoking and drug taking policy and the sanctions you will employ if it is abused.
- Allow plenty of time for questions and make sure you have all the answers (e.g. where the nearest hospital is, how much pocket money to take, what is covered in the insurance and so on).
- Be upbeat, confident and try to make the parents wish they were back at school and able to come along themselves.
- For younger pupils explain how you'll deal with homesickness.

Information from parents

You must get the following information from parents before you can allow their children to join you on your trip:

- Express permission for their son/daughter to join your trip and take part in all the activities (a signed and dated reply slip will normally allow this).
- Parents' or guardians' (next of kin) daytime and evening contact details.
- Details of any medical conditions or medication that the child may be taking while on your trip.
- Permission to act in the child's best interest if a medical emergency were to occur on an overnight trip and parents could not be contacted quickly enough.

Information from colleagues

We might work in the same school as the colleagues in our team, but we won't always know the pupils we're taking away. It's a good idea to gather information that could help us and our pupils get more out of a trip:

- Details of any behaviour problems or concerns, including disciplinary action taken – suspensions, exclusions, etc.
- Details of relationship issues – friendship group problems, romantic relationships, personality clashes, etc.
- Details of special learning needs.

Information for pupils

It's a good idea to provide pupils with some basic contact information should they get lost or need to get hold of help in an emergency. An **information card** with the following information will help:

- The destination of the trip hotel or museum name and phone number.
- The name of the party leader and a contact phone number – a mobile is best.
- The name of the school and a contact number.
- Instructions that explain what to do if the child gets lost or needs to contact you.
- Maybe also the name and number of the coach firm, or basic travel details and an itinerary.

Good communication practice

Try to share information as much as possible, but at times, where information is sensitive, you must operate a 'need to know' policy. It is important that key people are kept informed and that you maintain good records. Here are some suggestions for good communication practice:

- Use school mail-outs to parents or the school website to advertise the trips you will run that year.
- Make sure that pupils and parents are aware of your aims and objectives for your trip.
- Use a reply slip on your letter to parents and make sure it is worded in a way that makes it clear what the parents are agreeing to.
- Make public the *where, when, how* and *why* details about your trip.

- Organise to contact **one person** in the event of an emergency and make sure your team knows who this is.
- Copy the itinerary, list of pupils attending and your contact details while away to the school office, your emergency contact person and the staffroom. Why not provide a map of your destination or route?
- Try to get a noticeboard set aside in your staffroom specially for school trips.
- Copy relevant senior management in on emails and letters that go to parents.
- Set up email mailing lists once your team and pupil group is finalised – useful for residential trips.
- Once you receive payment in the form of a cheque from parents, send them a receipt or a booking confirmation letter.

> ### Why not try this?
>
> Send an update email to parents when you arrive at your destination and at a couple of regular intervals during the trip. It's easy to do by email in most places with wireless internet access now widely available. This not only keeps parents informed, but also allows them to share in part of their child's experience – they can talk about it with their children when they get home.

Management information systems and emailing

If you've got a good management information system (MIS) – not all are – and you can use it to create lists and send emails to groups of students' parents, then you should take advantage of this to help save time. A MIS will provide contact details, medical details, phone numbers and addresses for parents and so much more. All this information would take an age to collect and enter into a spreadsheet by hand.

Emailing and 'parent-mail' systems are the way forward. They are so much quicker and more reliable than sending letters home with pupils, which often get lost in school bags. Why not think about setting up text message alert systems too?

Mobile phones

You might not want to give out your mobile number to the children on your trip. But it's a good idea to give them an easy way of contacting you in an emergency. You can buy a pay as you go SIM card with a different number to your own and give this out so that the children can contact you. Put this SIM card in an old mobile and carry this and your own phone around on the trip. Just make sure you have enough credit on the card to allow you to call the kids back. You can budget for this before you go.

Inclusion, equality and behaviour

It is important that your trip is open to all as far as is possible. In some schools there may be policy that dictates how some children can be prevented from going on trips if their behaviour record has been poor. This is a good step to take if their previous behaviour has been seen to damage learning for others (it could be worse away from school). However, learning beyond the classroom can actually have a very positive effect on children who are poorly behaved in class, violent behaviour and language aside. It's a fine balance to strike.

It might help to think about equality and inclusion by making a number of assumptions about what we might feel is right, ethical and moral.

> All children deserve access to a balanced, varied and well-resourced education including opportunities to learn outside the classroom.

> Decisions about access to education on school trips should never be made based on a child's gender, race, health or cultural or religious beliefs.

We can be sure that most people would agree with the statements above. When planning a trip you might also want to consider your pupils' contexts very seriously. Think about the following questions in light of the previous assumptions:

> Could your planned trip activities exclude any group or individuals from taking part?

> Could the destination, content or context of your trip cause serious offence to any group or individuals who might take part?

You are more knowledgeable about your school's context and religious and cultural diversity, so you'll be aware of aspects of your practice where you need to be sensitive to the legitimate beliefs of others. That is not to say that you should avoid trips that expand your pupils' cultural awareness in case you upset a small group. Quite the opposite, but you'll want to be careful how you deal with the issues and how you pitch your trip.

Special physical needs and learning difficulties

Many children and young adults with special educational needs and learning difficulties receive their education in mainstream schools up and down the country. There are huge benefits to this practice for all concerned, but it does make planning a school trip a little more involved.

If you work in a school that integrates pupils with special physical needs or learning difficulties, you'll be well briefed on how to meet their needs during normal lessons. But you will need to think carefully about how to meet their needs when away from school.

Get together with your colleagues and work out protocols for planning and managing school trips in an inclusive way. Consider the following as starting points:

● Access to transport and buildings (wheelchair access and access to exhibits or activities).

● Care and supervision (staff/pupil ratios and appropriate training and qualifications).

● Appropriateness of the activities (inclusive activities that all can be involved in).

● Comfort of your pupils (special care for bathroom breaks or medication, rest and food).

One objective of any trip is to ensure that every pupil on it receives the same experience and has access to the same sensations and facilities as far as reasonably possible.

Reflecting on practice

When you last visited a museum or went on a school trip, how aware were you of facilities that allowed access and enjoyment for all?

How could you make your trips more inclusive?

What about adventurous activities and inclusion?

Children with special physical needs needn't be excluded from adventurous activities. Indeed, organisations like the Calvert Trust, based in Northumberland, Exmoor and the Lake District, are set up to cater for children and young adults of all abilities. They also offer respite care for families of young adults with special physical, sensory and/or learning needs.

They are fantastic places to spend a week and provide such a great experience for all who get involved, and are expert at providing truly inclusive activities. (See www.calvert-trust.org.uk.)

Why not try this?

Able-bodied children can enjoy a week of adventure sports alongside young people with special physical, sensory and /or learning needs. Activities are integrated and provide huge amounts of social capital for all concerned.

Think about including able-bodied children in the world of children with special needs, rather than the other way round.

Behaviour

Poor behaviour has been cited many times as one of the reasons that teachers do not want to continue to run school trips. While it is important to be inclusive, we must realise the damaging effect that some pupils can have when their behaviour is just not suitable for a given activity or environment.

However, we must never confuse disruptive behaviour with a special educational need. So where a pupil has a special need or a social interaction problem that manifests itself in difficult rather than intentionally disruptive behaviour, we must make every effort to continue to include them.

It might help to think about behaviour as a hazard in a risk assessment:

1. What is the hazard?
2. Who is at risk?
3. What control is in place?
4. What additional control might be required for the specific situation?

A pupil with a history of disruptive or abusive behaviour might present a hazard in the way they damage other pupils' learning while away from school. Existing control measures might not be suitable for an out-of-school situation. Additional measures might be needed, such as extra staff to help supervise a child or group of children.

However, you might decide that too many resources are tied up in providing one child or a minority of children with the experience of a school trip. Sad as this might be, you may have to make a pragmatic decision and think about the many over the few. This is perfectly acceptable, providing that you explain your reasons in writing and provide behaviour expectations in your original letter to parents. Remember, you are not obligated to run school trips, although they may be encouraged at your school. As with so many things, your decision making process should be as transparent as possible.

> ### Why not try this?
>
> Risk can arise from behaviour as much as it can from a hazardous activity. Whether the behaviour is intentional or not, you must weigh up the challenges that it presents to everyone's safety. For example, while for some children a trip to a water fowl nature reserve might not present any significant hazards, to children with behavioural problems a venue with unprotected water margins can represent a significant hazard.
>
> Include behaviour hazards in your risk assessment!

Excluding a pupil from a trip is a last resort following an unacceptable behaviour record. Yet, in some cases, getting difficult pupils out of the classroom into environments where they are less comfortable can be quite revealing and very productive, so don't automatically discount the difficult ones: treat each case on its merits. Here are some suggestions for good practice:

- Set out your behaviour policy early on – make it clear why you might need to exclude a pupil and on what terms you might re-include them.
- If you are charging for the trip, decide how/if you will refund a pupil if you decide to exclude them.
- If you exclude a pupil, decide how they will be supervised when they are left at school.
- Think about how excluded pupils will catch up on the learning they will miss.
- Finally, get your head teacher to agree your policy in writing at the planning stage.

Pupils will let you down from time to time, even the nicest kids. Accept this as a fact of life. Be prepared for bad behaviour and never take it personally – you're a professional!

Conclusion

Planning and inspiring others can actually be an enjoyable part of your trip. Whether it's a day trip or a longer residential trip, there can be some satisfaction from building and creating the learning experience you believe in.

Getting colleagues together to spread the load, distribute the leadership and collaborate on risk assessments and aims and objectives is an extremely satisfying part of the process. Other people have some fantastic ideas and can draw on a wealth of experience, but you must have the strength to keep them on track and follow your leadership. Don't forget that trips offer you a chance to grow beyond classroom teaching into proper leadership of people in an unfamiliar environment.

Don't misunderstand the advice that this chapter has presented. You could interpret things incorrectly, thinking that creating more paperwork is the answer. That's not the case at all. I've presented ideas here for sharing, collaborating and distributing roles, responsibilities and leadership aimed at lightening your load, while still being thorough and well organised.

Chapter 3 considers some ideas for getting to your destination and exploring the country around us. Transport is one of the areas where you can distribute leadership to a member of your team, or delegate the tasks of booking and communicating with commercial providers.

Key ideas summary

- Aims and objectives must be clearly defined and communicated to all.
- Build a good team.
- Use a system to organise your planning.
- Distribute and delegate leadership.
- Use checklists and know your responsibilities.
- Use risk assessments as part of the planning meeting process – do them collaboratively.
- Visit the site if you can.
- Use the trip for teacher learning as well as pupil learning.
- Don't try to do too much on one trip – keep things simple.
- Adapt your teaching style when on a trip – what works in the classroom might not work in the field.
- Good communication is essential for all concerned. You need to communicate well with parents and colleagues, but they must also communicate well with you.
- Use technology that makes communication easy for you.
- Budget carefully.
- Be completely transparent where money is concerned and keep excellent records.
- Consider equality, inclusion and behaviour carefully.

Going further

Websites

For school travel:

www.schooltravelforum.com

Health and safety and risk assessments:

www.teachernet.gov.uk/wholeschool/healthandsafety/visits/

For learning outside the classroom:

www.outdoor-learning.org

www.lotc.org.uk

For dealing with behaviour:

www.behaviouronline.com

Further reading

Andrews, K. (2001) *Extra Learning: New opportunities for the out of school hours* (London: Kogan Page).

Boud, D., Cohen, R. and Walker, D. (eds) (1993) *Using Experience for Learning* (Buckingham: Open University Press).

Cline, T. and Frederickson, N. (2009) *Special Educational Needs, Inclusion and Diversity*, 2nd edn (Maidenhead: Open University).

Davies, S. (2006) *The Essential Guide to Teaching* (Harlow: Pearson).

DfES (2002) *Handbook for Group Leaders* (Nottingham: DfES).

DfES (2002) *Standards for Adventure Part 2* (Nottingham: DfES).

DfES (1998) *Health and Safety of Pupils on Educational Visits* (Nottingham: DfES).

Dix, P. (2007) *Taking Care of Behaviour* (Harlow: Pearson).

Glenn, A., Cousins, J. and Helps, A. (2004) *Behaviour in the Early Years: Tried and tested strategies* (London: David Fulton).

Griffin, S. (2008) *Inclusion, Equality and Diversity in Working with Children* (Harlow: Pearson).

Gronn, P. (2000) Distributed Properties: A new architecture for leadership, *Educational Management and Administration*, 28 (3), 317–38.

→

Kemshall, H and Pritchard, J. (1988) *Good Practice in Risk Assessment and Risk Management* (London: Jessica Kingsley).

Kolb, D. (1984) *Experiential Learning: Experience as the source of learning and development* (Englewood Cliffs, NJ: Prentice-Hall).

Morris, S. (2006) *Spreadsheets with Excel* (Oxford: Butterworth-Heinemann).

Rogers, B. (2007) *Behaviour Management: A whole school approach* (London: Sage).

Spilane, J. (2006) *Distributed Leadership* (San Francisco, CA: Jossey-Bass).

For action practitioner action research techniques:

Carr, W. and Kemmis, S. (1986) *Becoming Critical* (Lewes: Farmer).

Denzin, N. and Lincoln, Y. (eds) *Handbook of Qualitative Research* (London: Sage).

Relevant research studies

Anderson, D., Kisiel, J. and Storksdiek, M. (2006) Understanding Teachers' Perspectives on Fieldtrips: Discovering common ground in three countries, *Curator: The Museum Journal*, 49 (3), 365–386.

Anderson, D. and Zhang, Z. (2003) Teacher Perceptions of Field-Trip Planning and Implementation, *Visitor Studies Today*, 6 (3), 6–11.

Bailie, M. (2006) Risk Assessments, Safety Statements and all that, *Horizons Magazine* (Institute of Outdoor Learning), winter 2006, issue 36, 13–15.

Kisiel, J. (2005) Understanding Elementary Teacher Motivations for Science Fieldtrips, *Science Education*, 89 (6), 936–955.

Xanthoudaki, M. (1998) Is It Always Worth the Trip? The contribution of museum and gallery education programmes to classroom art education, *Cambridge Journal of Education*, 28 (2), 181–195.

Chapter

3

How to get there

What this chapter will explore:

- Different methods of transport
- Associated benefits and problems
- Convenience, cost and safety

The method of travel you use will have some effect on the children's and adults' enjoyment of the trip. Some children may never have travelled on certain forms of transport (the London Underground is a good example), and this may prove a key aspect of the trip that helps to unlock other memories later on. I remember taking a taxi-boat across to Venice with a large group of pupils on our way back from a trip in northern Italy. The boat trip provided further adventure and excitement for the group and turned what is often a dull journey home into something more special.

Often, your trip will involve a hired coach or a school minibus, but you needn't stick to these if your school has good access to the railway, bus or tube/metro system. If you are travelling abroad your choices might be more limited, but try not to ignore the possibility of public transport as an alternative to a hired coach as it is often extremely enlightening and enjoyable and exposes your group to more experiences. Just recently I paid €20, about £12 at the time of writing, to take 20 teenage pupils and three adults from Salzburg city centre to the airport. The buses were prompt and clean and the journey really very enjoyable. It gave us a chance to chat to fellow passengers, practise language skills, enjoy the scenery and interact with the city in a way that a private coach wouldn't have allowed. So although we often reach for the coach hire company's phone number or take a minibus almost as a default action, we could add further value to the trip by being creative with our travel arrangements. Indeed for younger staff who aren't old enough to drive a minibus, or for smaller groups of pupils, the train or bus might be the better option.

Minibuses

Most schools have some form of access to a minibus – whether it is a local authority share scheme or a fleet of brand new buses, it doesn't matter. What matters is that they are used, and that they are used well and safely.

I have to confess that I'm a fan of minibuses and love driving them around the country on expeditions and subject trips. If you enjoy driving, they represent a new and interesting challenge. They are much bigger than your family car and in many ways your cargo is the most valuable you will ever carry – other people's children – so they present a professional challenge as well. There's more to driving a minibus than kicking the tyres, firing it up and zooming off to your destination. Here are a few points for your consideration.

Rest

Never drive a minibus if you are tired. If you feel yourself becoming weary, roll down the window, find a place to rest and take refreshment. Better to be 30 minutes late than not arrive at all. Consider the following tips:

- Never drive for longer than two hours without a stop.
- Plan rest stops into a long trip.
- When you stop, take a walk and have a drink of juice, water or a maximum of two cups of coffee.
- Don't eat too much if you stop. If you do eat, avoid heavy carbohydrate meals and allow time to digest.

- Try not to overdo the stimulant drinks – they can affect your judgement and perception of speed and distance.

Fuel

Most minibuses use diesel; sounds obvious, I know, but many has been the time when colleagues of mine have happily filled a diesel with petrol and vice versa. It's not the end of the world but whichever mistake you make, don't drive off if you realise while at the pump. Call your breakdown assistance service and get it sorted.

Parking

Parking a large vehicle that you don't drive every day can be daunting, especially in a busy town or city. Try to avoid busy car parks; go for sensible parking and take it slow. Do your homework and work out exactly where you are going to park before you leave. Make sure that valuables and belongings of any sort are out of sight or locked away. Here are some other suggestions:

- Never use parking meters – they'll cost more than your trip.
- Try getting in touch with the school nearest to your destination – they might be happy to help you out with a parking space, and you can always return the favour one day.

Congestion Charge

If you venture into the centre of London then you'll be liable for the Congestion Charge. This makes travelling by rail, tube or bus more attractive in this particular city, but it's not always the best option when you have younger children with you unless you have sufficient chaperones. Many other cities are considering congestion charge type schemes so it's something we are going to have to deal with more and more.

Motorways

These are great for covering distance efficiently but can be challenging and intimidating for some. The key here is observation and anticipation, especially if you are driving a speed restricted vehicle (often restricted by limiting revs in particular gears making acceleration tricky if you are already at top speed). You must drive to maintain a safe speed while observing well ahead and behind to anticipate overtaking manoeuvres that you or other road users might make.

Never stop on the hard shoulder except in an emergency. If you do, follow the advice for a breakdown (see below).

Breakdown

It's going to happen at some point – because you've run out of fuel or there is some other technical gremlin. If it does happen, you need to have a plan:

- If you break down follow the school's set protocol.
- Stop somewhere where you have good vision of the road ahead and behind you.
- Pull well in to the safe side of the hard shoulder.
- Evacuate your vehicle on the safe side of the hard shoulder – don't use rear doors.
- Move your pupils up the embankment and well to the rear of your vehicle.
- If your vehicle is hit by another passing vehicle the debris will travel forward of your pupils, not towards them.
- In bad weather, ensure that your party is protected from the elements somehow.
- Call the school office to let them know what's happened.
- Call your breakdown assistance service. Don't be tempted to do anything like changing a tyre on a busy road.
- If you can't carry on for any reason, get your school to arrange alternative transport (get them working for you).
- Don't be tempted to get your credit card out to sort the problem unless it's the last resort.

Country lanes

The innocuous country lane has been the undoing of many a minibus driver. When driving in narrow lanes your attention needs to be extremely focused. Often you will need to pull in close to a hedge to allow a farm vehicle to pass or even reverse to a passing space. Your other concern is livestock, which can either be driven down tracks by farmers or escape from fields with little warning.

Some good general advice

- Get some training.
- Drive smoothly – make every gear change a joy to experience.

- Brake progressively – slow down in good time; brake so smoothly that your passengers can't even tell you've stopped. Don't forget that braking distances are significantly *increased* in the wet and that ABS is not a magic system – so don't rely on it alone.

- Observe – look out for hazards well ahead and road signs that can inform your progress.

- Anticipate – what's going on ahead and behind, how could it affect you, and how will you take action? Have an escape route.

- Plan – know where you are going and how you are going to get there. Have an alternative route too.

Local authorities now run minibus driver training schemes that all drivers need to pass if they want to operate 16-seater buses while on LA/school business. So all maintained schools should have staff that fall into this category. The situation with independent schools is often different, but in most cases your school governing body will insist that these LA driving assessments are taken *and passed* by all staff who want or need to use minibuses. Most of these tests need to be renewed on a three-yearly basis, so you need to keep up to date with good practice on the roads in that time. But you need to be aware of the law too.

Minibus driving and the law

You can start driving minibuses from the age of 21 providing you have passed the necessary test and hold D1 entitlement on your driving licence. However, insuring you at 21 is a different matter: most companies will only insure you if you are over 25.

Driving standards at home and abroad
If you want to drive abroad then you must also pass a version of the PSV (Public Service Vehicles) test which entails using tachographs and covers the specific needs of driving abroad. It will include content on speed limits, the law, braking and use of gears, observation and anticipation. Depending on your instructor you may also be taught basic maintenance and emergency procedures.

Speed limits
Do different speed limits apply to minibuses? Some buses are actually restricted to 65mph, but the same speed limits apply to minibuses as to cars. Always drive within the speed limit. Imagine how you'd be treated by a police officer if you were caught speeding with kids on board – not sympathetically!

Seatbelts and safety
By law, you must wear a seatbelt in cars, minibuses, vans and goods vehicles where one is fitted. Younger children will require help and a different type

→

Minibus driving and the law continued

of child restraint if they weigh less than 36kg and are less than 135cm tall. Following a child's twelfth birthday they may wear an adult seatbelt.

In buses and coaches with seatbelts fitted, passengers older than three years of age should use adult seatbelts unless a booster child restraint is available. Fare paying passengers travelling in public vehicles on 30mph roads are exempt from using seatbelts.

According to the Department for Transport (www.dft.gov.uk/think/focusareas/children), it is the passenger's responsibility to wear a seatbelt if they are over 14 years of age, not yours. But do you think a police officer would let you off on that count? Not likely!

If you're going to travel by road, make sure you use the safety devices available.

Mobile phones and distractions
Do not use mobile phones while driving. If you need to make a call, get a passenger to make it for you or stop somewhere safe.

Drinking and driving
No debate here – don't do it. Alcohol can still impair your driving the morning after you've had a drink. No excuses, if you're driving a minibus the following day don't drink the night before.

Roof racks and luggage and trailers
You are responsible for ensuring that any load fitted to the outside of your vehicle is secure and won't cause a hazard to other road users. Also be aware of your maximum height when your roof rack is full. Make sure your trailer is safely connected and that all lights work and a correct number plate is fitted. Loads should not obscure lights, mirrors or number plates.

Reflecting on practice

How do you feel about the responsibility involved in driving a minibus? Do you relish it or resent it?

Does your school have a policy on minibus use? A training scheme? Even an expectation of what condition to leave a minibus in when you've finished?

Have you been on your local LA's training scheme? Was it useful and are you a better driver now?

What tips might you pass on if you've got lots of experience of driving minibuses?

Trains

Despite the rising cost of tickets in the UK in recent times, the train is by far a better option than the public bus. Group tickets are easier to purchase and greater distances can be covered more conveniently. Trains really should be our first choice for long-distance travel in the UK as they offer a more environmentally friendly option and a convenient alternative to the charter coach if a station is close to your school. Further, the option to combine travel by train, tube and tram or bus in larger cities provides you with a great deal of flexibility on your trip and superb value if you really get around.

For small groups the train can be an excellent option – indeed my economics colleagues run an annual trip to Brussels by Eurostar and swear by its efficiency and ease of use. And that's the key here – you've got to choose the transport option that is most convenient for you and your party. You've got to think about how you can manage your group, their age and abilities, and where you're going.

When considering travelling by train, remember the following:

- As with flying, sea travel and scheduled bus services, trains are public spaces. Expect to interact and deal with unexpected situations.
- It's amazingly easy to get lost on the Underground, metro or subway. Plan to count your group through each and every turnstile.

Reflecting on practice

Try to think of your current professional setting. Could you use trains for your own trips? What might make your life difficult?

What might the benefits be for you?

If you've used trains before how do your experiences resonate with what you've read?

What tips might you pass on?

Buses and coaches

Public transport buses

It's pretty unlikely that your trip will involve a great deal of bus travel, but if you do use the bus you might be surprised at how easy it is. In the UK buses don't have a great reputation for punctuality and quality of service and, to be honest, I've always found them to be rather expensive for what you get. However, buses can provide a useful option, particularly used in conjunction with rail or air travel. There are a number of problems with bus travel though:

- Your party won't always get a seat.
- Pupils are easy to lose when getting on and off a busy and noisy bus.
- Buses can be expensive.
- Tickets are difficult to purchase for large groups in the UK.

Charter coaches

Good coach-hire companies are worth establishing a 'preferred provider' relationship with if your school can do this. However, driver temperament can play an unnecessarily negative part in your trip on occasion. I hate it when somebody treats kids as though they are all the same and just out to wreck things and behave badly. For some reason it's been my experience that some coach drivers suffer from this delusion. Conversely, a good driver can really add to the atmosphere of your trip.

A 22-hour trip to the Alps is not for the unprepared or naive. Nevertheless, it can be easier than getting on and off aeroplanes and allows a bigger baggage weight limit. On the other hand, if you do use a coach as your main form of travel for a week's trip skiing or on an adventure tour of the Ardeche valley, for example, you'll have to ensure that the drivers (there'll be two if you are on long journeys) get on with the group. They'll have to gel with you and your staff.

Coach driving and the law

- Coach drivers must stick rigidly to 'their hours'.
- Drivers of passenger carrying vehicles in the EU must drive for no more than nine hours a day, and no longer than four and a half hours in one session, which must be followed by a break of at least 45 minutes.
- On a long trip, a second driver could take over at a stop after the first 4.5 hours to allow the first driver to take a break while still travelling.
- Outside the EU there may not be any laws pertaining to driving hours or seatbelt safety – it depends where you go, so you must check travel arrangements carefully.
- If you suspect anything out of the ordinary – drivers going too long without a break, using mobile phones, etc., you must take a deep breath and politely mention it at the time. If the situation feels wrong to you, then do what you need to do – you're the customer and you're in charge. It is better to cause upset and embarrassment than to allow a situation that might result in an accident.

Travel sickness

Thankfully this is rarer these days than I, and many of my colleagues, remember from our own childhoods. Air conditioning and temperature control probably have something to do with this, and perhaps improved visibility on coaches and buses too. As with sea sickness, there is a school of thought that if you can look straight ahead it will help to calm the stomach and reduce sickness. Of course, travel sickness occurs more in young children who tend to sit well below the head level of the seats and so can't see forward. Here are some suggestions to try to avoid travel sickness:

● Get children who are travel sick to sit at the front so they can see where they are going.
● Try keeping the temperature at a comfortable level – not too hot and with some movement of air.
● Peppermints, barley sugar and ginger nut biscuits can help.
● Keep a couple of sick bags, packets of tissues and wet wipes in your day sack too.

Reflecting on practice

For domestic journeys weigh up the pros and cons of bus/coach or train travel. What scenarios make one more appropriate than the other?

If you take a regular trip to a destination, why not try a different method of transport next time?

Flying

More and more schools are taking advantage of long-haul destinations for large-scale expeditions and tours. Rugby tours to Japan are more common than you'd think, as are expeditions to the Chilean Andes. Long-haul destinations aren't restricted to children of senior school age either and more independent school travel companies offer trips to destinations in the USA, Canada and Australia. Clearly there are higher costs involved in this sort of travel that may prevent a good number of children from less advantaged backgrounds taking part without considerable fundraising activities.

Low cost airlines

If you leave baggage out of the equation, travelling by air is actually very straight-forward, and it offers a wider range of destinations for your trip. A good many

Duke of Edinburgh's Award Gold candidates from the south of England have taken advantage of cheap flights to travel to Scotland for their assessed expeditions recently; the flight is only just an hour and can get you to the mountains quickly. However, flying can provide you with more organisational problems if you don't think ahead.

Group passports

Your party will need to carry and look after their own passports for at least part of the journey unless you organise a group passport (see www.ips.gov.uk/passport/collective.asp). This requires a little more organising for the group leader but means that groups of between five and 50 can travel without the need for individual passports as long as the adult in charge has held a full British passport for over ten years and is travelling with the group. Problems might occur if pupils drop out of the trip and are replaced at short notice, but it's worth considering as an alternative to individual passports.

Marshalling your group through the airport

Have a plan!

You arrive at check-in and a member of your staff checks the group in; another member goes through the security and counts your group through and then heads to the gate. If you inform the security people first they'll often open a lane especially for you, particularly if you are travelling with young children or young people with special needs (doing your homework and contacting the airport first might help).

When at the gate the airline staff will count your group in and then again when seated. Your group will be counted around ten times by a combination of you, your staff and the airport staff. In theory, you shouldn't be able to lose anyone as they'll get a public address call if they don't make it to the gate. Well, that's the theory anyway; of course you can lose children anywhere, but there are ways to help prevent it – the classic 'buddy-buddy' system is well used.

If opting to travel by air, reflect on the following suggestions:

- Decide whether you are meeting your tour party at the airport or travelling together.
- Have your team organised before you get to the airport – each person should know their job.
- Split bigger parties into smaller groups with a member of staff or senior pupil in charge of each one.
- Whenever you move off from somewhere or stop somewhere, check with your group leaders to see if everyone is present.

- Give all staff a list of names and parent contact details. Put someone in charge of checking passports and bags.
- Station a member of staff on the check-in desk.
- Check one member of staff in first and ask them to go through security and check pupils off a list as they come through. They should make themselves known to security staff and explain that a school group is coming through.
- Arrange pupils to meet this member of staff and muster at an agreed point – this may be the gate or an area of the departure lounge.
- When boarding, introduce yourself to cabin crew as the member of staff in charge of the school party on board.
- Wear something easily identifiable – my pupils often think I'm daft for wearing a flat cap and a Hawaiian shirt when we fly, but I'm easy to find in a crowd when they need me.

Reflecting on practice

Consider how you would view your professional behaviour and the behaviour of your pupils when out in public. Think of a recent example and reflect on how you might come across and whether you could adjust your practice or your pupils' behaviour for the better. Also reflect on good comments you've received from members of the public – what did you/your pupils do that made an impact?

Travelling on water

Small boats and canoes

It is possible that you might choose this method of transport as an end in itself – a canoeing activity or as part of a Duke of Edinburgh's Award expedition. Many schools routinely run canoeing and sailing activities with their own qualified staff, while others rely on outdoor pursuits centres for expert instruction and supervision. Whichever route is taken, it is ultimately down to the head teacher to ensure that staff working with pupils are appropriately trained and experienced and, of course, have passed a CRB (Criminal Records Bureau) check if needed.

If you are to engage in water based activities with children, you have to be qualified and experienced, and you'd expect all your pupils to wear life jackets – right? As with most activities there is always the exception that proves the rule, so would you expect the above to apply to a sixth form punting trip to

Cambridge? Punting in Cambridge is a central feature of the character of the city and university, and a trip to experience either would, arguably, be incomplete without a punt along the Cam.

If you're taking this sort of trip you are unlikely to take a qualified person along or ask everyone to wear life jackets as it would detract from the enjoyment and the authenticity of the experience. The utility of the event would be lost and prove an embarrassing memory for your pupils. If you had a younger group with you then life jackets and a higher level of supervision would be a good way forward, but for older kids this might not be appropriate or necessary.

- Any adventurous activity such as canoeing or sailing must be run by qualified and experienced professionals with an instructor/pupil ratio that is accepted by the activity's governing body.
- Remember that not being an expert at something doesn't prevent you from making an informed and common sense judgement – if you have a concern you must share it.
- Your responsibility is to ensure that the staff you use or the outdoor centres that you go to are qualified, fully licensed and well respected.
- Delegate the hands-on instruction but make sure that all instructors know who you are and what you expect – don't interfere in their work though (unless you feel that safety is being compromised).
- If you have worries about an instructor, talk to their superior discreetly – no need to worry your pupils.
- On longer activity trips you should arrange regular meetings with the instructors so you can all share information.
- Do your homework covering qualifications, training standards and safety procedures – this will enable you to make informed decisions about activities.
- Pull the plug if you feel what is going on doesn't match with your expectations.

Despite these cautionary words, it must be said that these activities offer a huge amount of utility for groups and individuals alike and allow the development of physical and psychological strength in young adults especially.

Ships and ferries

Ships and ferries actually pose a number of interesting questions over supervision and safety. Because of their size it might be worth thinking of them in the same way you would when on a trip in an unfamiliar town. If you are on a ship for more than a couple of hours you'll need to think carefully about your safety procedures and your group management. As on an aeroplane, the captain has overall responsibility for the passengers on the vessel, but you can't just wander on to a ferry and wash your hands of your group, citing 'maritime law' as your reason for putting your feet up in the lounge. You are still responsible for your group, their behaviour and their safety.

Behaviour in any public place can be the undoing of any good trip unless ground rules are discussed and agreed right at the start. The last part, 'agreed', is really very important and can't be understated. Explain the rules, give good reason and ask for agreement. Give anyone who disagrees or wants to challenge the rules an opportunity to do so. Not only does this give the impression of democracy and fairness, it actually *is* democratic and fair if you take on board your group's concerns, should they have any.

Here are some more suggestions:

- Arrange a regular meet point for roll calls during the crossing or voyage.
- With younger children, supervise more closely. Have activities that will take up most of the crossing.
- Know the muster stations and have an idea of the exits and how you and your staff will deal with problems.
- Brief your pupils about slippery decks and how to behave outside
- Be prepared for sea sickness!
- Inform the purser that you have a school group on board and give them your contact details.

Reflecting on practice

Consider the circumstances of a journey over water. Under what circumstances would you:

- Allow free time?
- Expect your pupils to gather in one place?
- Allow access to shops or 'duty-free'?
- Set 'out of bounds' areas?

How would you and your staff appropriately supervise the group – split them up, keep them together, use senior pupils as monitors or give them free time?

Would you collect mobile numbers (with parents' permission) for contacting latecomers?

Cars

Many teachers up and down the country regularly use their own private cars to transport pupils to sports fixtures, extra-curricular activities or hospital A&E departments. Using your own car is quick, simple and convenient, but it could leave you open to a number of obvious, and not so obvious, problems.

First, you might need to be insured to use your car for business purposes. Any costs incurred by you for insuring your car for this purpose will rarely be covered by your school, so think carefully about this before travelling. Some schools do include the use of teachers' cars in their own insurance policies, but this is by no means common practice, so check with your bursar, health and safety officer or educational visits coordinator (EVC).

Do you have parental permission for pupils to travel in your car and, if so, for what specific purpose? You must also be aware of the need to consider child safety matters. Is it really professional for you to be alone with a pupil in your car? Many unions would advise against transporting pupils in private vehicles altogether, but there are many dilemmas that crop up that might force you to make a difficult decision. However, as with most issues covered in this book, you should be able to avoid problems by planning sufficiently. Here is a summary of what you should consider before using your own car:

- Will my insurance cover it?
- Will the school's insurance cover it?
- Do I have the head's permission?
- Do I have parental permission?
- Is my car up to the job – is it safe (MOT)?
- What about the suitability of the seatbelts – do I need a booster seat? What is the law (see page 67)?
- How can I ensure my own professional safety?
- Who's paying for the fuel?

If you can answer these questions to your own satisfaction and that of the school then it might not be a problem. But the final decision must be made with all factors considered carefully before you start.

Reflecting on practice

If you've used your own car to transport pupils before, consider why you've needed to do so. Has it been a last minute solution to a planning problem, a permanent arrangement or a planned solution to transporting a very small group? Has it caused you any problems or anxieties?   →

Have you spent your own money? Do you always claim your expenses back correctly?

If you are serious about encouraging learning away from school, is using your own car a sustainable solution?

Bicycles

When I started teaching I was told of a schoolmaster who used to lead outings by bicycle. Try to imagine an eccentric character cycling through the Hertfordshire countryside with boys in short trousers and caps eagerly following on behind on their way to see Henry Moore and his studios at Perry Green. On arrival they met the great man himself who took them on a tour of the sculpture gardens and various sheds full of artists' treasures before they enjoyed a picnic in the grounds and made their way back to their boarding houses. This peek into a 1950s boarding school education is closer to the Harry Potter stories than to the reality of school trips today. But doesn't it sound delightful even so?

Despite this, you are unlikely to want to travel by bicycle with a group of children in tow for very good reasons, most probably linked to health and safety issues or just the sheer effort involved. Nevertheless, you might find that cycling forms part of an adventure holiday, or a Duke of Edinburgh's Award expedition. At the time of writing the British government was even considering introducing cycle safety into the school curriculum, so many of us might not have any choice in the matter.

Walking

In many ways, those that can go on an educational visit by walking are the luckiest, and are most likely set in a city centre. Cities provide a huge wealth of destinations for school trips. The concentration of museums, galleries, theatres, parks, zoos and other assorted attractions means that teachers are almost spoilt for choice. Walking is the cheapest option for any trip and means that planning can be kept to a minimum, but you need to be aware of a range of roadside hazards.

Group management – how will you control your group? Younger children may hold hands and walk in twos with adults spread intermittently along the group, but older children will resent anything like this. So think carefully about your group.

Roads with paths – remember that the general public will want to pass by on the same path. Being considerate of the general public should always be one of your priorities.

Roads without paths – dodgy one this. Many organisations who regularly walk along roads with no paths have very strict codes of practice for this. Leaders and rear-markers might wear hi-visibility jackets, carry lit torches at night and maintain strict single file walking towards the flow of traffic so you can see what's coming at you. That said, it's best to plan sufficiently to avoid this sort of thing if you possibly can.

> Can you remember the teacher/pupil ratios?
>
> What's the best way of crossing roads with a large group of children? Have a look at Figure 4.1 on p107 for an idea.

Of course, walking will form the greater part of most Duke of Edinburgh's Award expeditions and this should be borne in mind. Although such expeditions are supposed to avoid travelling *along* roads, it is possible that the group you are supervising may need to use one as an escape route if something goes wrong.

Reflecting on practice

Some organisations go over the top with health and safety and insist that children wear hi-visibility jackets whenever they go near a road. Some might say there is nothing more hideous and unnecessary. A great deal of health and safety is down to sensible interpretation.

What's your philosophy on health and safety?

Safety is as much about culture as it is about wearing bright colours and avoiding fun things in life, so how do you manage risk without restricting freedom?

Cost, convenience and safety

When it comes down to making a decision about getting to your destination, the three factors of cost, convenience and safety should start off your decision making process nicely. Of course, context makes a huge impact on your decision too. You may not be working in an area of the country populated by people with large disposable incomes, but that shouldn't stop you from making the most of the opportunity to get out and engage in teaching and learning using what surrounds you. Education outside the classroom needn't be costly, but transporting your pupils to and from a destination can be. There may well be funds available that can be used to help and your EVC should be able to guide you in that direction. Parent teacher organisations (PTAs) raise a great deal of money for such activities and are an excellent source of support more generally.

> **TOP TIP!**
>
> *Don't let cost put you off! Search around for grants and donations from trusts and local charities and businesses.*

Safety must be your prime concern, but it must not overshadow your trip, nor must you overstress it, particularly with nervous or apprehensive youngsters. When travelling, one of your key safety concerns involves group control and management. Controlling your group is not as straightforward as you might think; you can't herd children in the way you might want, but if you approach the issue of group safety sensibly you can avoid all sorts of problems. Chapter 4 deals with concerns over freedom and control and looks at four systems for managing a group of school children – high profile control, low profile control, the buddy-buddy system and remote supervision.

The first time you consider the safety aspects of a particular mode of travel, no matter where you are going, will probably be when you undertake a risk assessment and inspection visit. When you do, consider the convenience of your chosen method of travel for you, as well as for the pupils. A slower journey might offer greater convenience for you and your staff in terms of supervision, flexibility and luggage allowance than a quicker method.

Conclusion

After reading this chapter you should have an idea of the travel options open to you and some of the possible problems you might encounter. The method of travel that you choose is up to you, but you'll have to weigh up the pros and cons of your decision. You'll need to be able to justify it to senior members of staff, parents, governors and others in terms of suitability, safety and educational merit. Don't forget that the journey to your destination is not just a means to an end; it can also be part of your aims and objectives for the educational experience you engage in.

Key ideas summary

- Each method of travel has its own unique challenges – be aware of them.
- Make travelling part of the experience, even an aspect of one of your learning objectives.
- Be creative.
- Have a plan. Have a plan B, then a plan C – what if your minibus breaks down?
- Consider cost, safety and convenience before you decide your travel plans.
- Don't rule out public transport – go for 'group rate' tickets.
- Assess the risks of your chosen transport method carefully.
- Be aware of key legal issues, such as seatbelts, insurance, minibus driving regulations, coach drivers' hours, speed limits, etc.
- Plan how you'll move around with your group – getting on and off buses, boats, planes etc. Think about headcounts.

Going further

Websites

For general travel advice:

www.fco.gov.uk

www.schooltravelforum.com

www.fitfortravel.nhs.uk

www.hpa.org.uk

Minibuses:

www.dft.gov.uk/think/focusareas/children

www.hertsdirect.org/envroads/roadstrans/rsu/driving/advice/minibus/minibusguide1

www.dsa.gov.uk/ (Driving Standards Agency)

www.dvla.gov.uk/ (Driver and Vehicle Licensing Agency)

www.direct.gov.uk/en/Motoring/DriverLicensing/WhatCanYouDriveAndYourObligations/

www.vosa.gov.uk/ (Vehicle Operator Services Agency)

www.nasuwt.org.uk

www.brake.org.uk/

www.rospa.com/RoadSafety/resources/teachers.htm

Trains:

www.nationalrail.co.uk/

Buses and coaches:

www.traveline.org.uk/index.htm (Guild of British Coach Operators)

www.vosa.gov.uk/ (Vehicle Operator Services Agency)

Flying:

www.caa.co.uk/ (Civil Aviation Authority)

www.caa.co.uk/default.aspx?catid=6 (Air passenger consumer rights)

Small boats, canoes and water sports:

www.rya.org.uk (Royal Yachting Association)

www.bcu.org.uk/ (British Canoe Union)

www.pyb.co.uk/courses/ (Plas-y-Brenin, National Mountain Centre – for BCU training courses)

www.lifesavers.org.uk

Travelling at sea:

www.mcga.gov.uk/ (Maritime and Coastguard Agency)

Using your own car:

www.nasuwt.org.uk

www.teachers.org.uk (NUT)

www.brake.org.uk

Cycling:

www.bsca.org.uk/ (British Schools Cycling Association)

www.britishcycling.org.uk

www.rospa.com/RoadSafety/resources/teachers.htm

Walking:

www.rospa.com/RoadSafety/resources/teachers.htm

Further reading

DfES (2002) *Group safety at water margins* (Nottingham: DfES).

DfES (2002) *Handbook for Group Leaders* (Nottingham: DfES).

DfES (2002) *Standards for Adventure Part 2* (Nottingham: DfES).

DfES (1998) *Health and Safety of Pupils on Educational Visits* (Nottingham: DfES).

FCO and Lonely Planet (2006) *Travel Safe: Know before you go* (London: Lonely Planet).

Gray, W. (2007) *Travel with Kids* (London: Footprint).

RoSPA (1998) *Essential Minibus Driving,* 4th edn (London: RoSPA).

Wheeler, M. and Lanigan, C. (2002) *Travel with Children – Lonely Planet Guides* (London: Lonely Planet).

Leadership in practice, or practising leadership?

What this chapter will explore:

- Styles of leadership
- How not to lead
- Being positive
- Freedom or control?
- Practical leadership – who's in charge here?
- Protocols for distributing practical leadership

In Chapter 2, issues of leadership in planning were looked at from the perspective of a leader who is 'organising' others and setting out a rationale. This chapter suggests that there is more to it than mere organisational skills and, very importantly, that leadership is a changing, fluid activity.

School trips – what's in it for us?

Much of the research into school effectiveness and school improvement has placed huge emphasis on the quality of leadership and its relation to the performance of children in their learning. Mostly the research identifies senior leaders as key players in this role and it has tried to pin down exactly what it is about leadership that helps to create an effective school, or encourages a school to improve. But senior leaders don't become senior leaders without developing leadership abilities earlier in their careers. So, how can school trips help you build capacity in your own leadership?

Assuming that you are a progressive teacher and keen to improve practice in order to achieve future effective learning scenarios, you'll want to know what 'leadership' actually looks like during a school trip or visit. For some it's a simple question with simple answers. People who think of themselves as leaders might describe how they lead in an attempt to explain what sort of leadership is right for a given situation. Which of the following statements might you most connect with?

> I'm a leader; I provide opportunities for learning and tell people how they can learn better.

> I'm a leader because I have the experience and the knowledge to get pupils good grades if they follow my example.

> I'm a leader because I'm in a position of responsibility: people rely on me to make the right decisions.

> I'm a leader because I'm in charge; people do as I say because I have the experience to know best.

These descriptions seem to get progressively top heavy; they assume that leadership is all about getting others to follow. Perhaps our perception of leadership in schools has been coloured by recent emphasis by governments and authorities across the world on 'outcomes': examination results, league tables, university entrance figures and school inspection reports. Professor John MacBeath suggests that these confining structures, placed around teachers and pupils, restrict freedom to develop vision and curriculum leadership opportunities:

> *'In recognition of the tightly defined curriculum and assessment pathway, schools have increasingly looked more to open "extra" curricular spaces in which leadership and learning may be engaged.'*

> (MacBeath, 2008: 118)

Finding opportunities for teachers and pupils to engage in sustained leadership is problematic within these structures and can lead to rather contrived scenarios being created for leadership training – you'll know this if you've ever been on one of those dreadful 'leadership courses' where you do a lot of talking and not much else.

One important idea in this book is that school trips of all varieties provide excellent opportunities for leadership *practise* and leadership *practice*: not only for teachers, but also for pupils. The mere fact of being away from school seems somehow to heighten pupils' and teachers' awareness of the need for control, command and direction. Of course, a trip is an excellent opportunity for the mischievous too. The physical separation from school means that the party leader is at the top of the hierarchy tree. The buck stops there! This can be an empowering and satisfying experience for some, but daunting for others. In teaching today, there are few other opportunities to develop real leadership skills over a sustained period of time. School trips offer a concentrated opportunity to fine-tune and develop those skills like no other aspect of school life.

As you read on, you'll get an appreciation of a number of issues involved in leading school trips and, hopefully, an understanding of how your skills can develop and be sustained.

Styles of leadership

Are you a leader or a follower, a hero or a collaborator?

Often, when applying for a new job in teaching, particularly in a management role, the 'person specification' might list 'proven leadership skills' or 'team player' as qualities that the employer wants to find in the successful applicant. But what are leadership skills and how do you prove you've got them? And if you're a 'team player' you must be following a captain, so how could you do both?

Proving your leadership ability is hard to do, unless you can demonstrate it in a real situation. Your way of leading might be extremely effective, but may lack the performance and wow factor that some people might expect. This is where the issue of style comes into play. My style will always be different from yours, and it should be – I'm a different person. Leader or follower? It all depends on context.

Much work has been done to try to understand leadership in schools, and a number of styles of leadership have been observed which have proven to have had some impact (positive and negative) on school effectiveness and improvement. They are:

Heroic – one person leads from the front on the big issues.

Charismatic – personality is important; larger than life individuals who might inspire followership.

Authoritarian – requires obedience and conformity.

Moral – awareness of the big picture with altruistic intentions.

Visionary – inspirational individuals or teams with clear goals to achieve.

Principle centred – guided by ideals, philosophies and principles in decision making and planning.

Professional – by example and to achieve expected levels of competence, ethics and behaviour.

Strategic – similar to visionary, looking at how to systematically achieve the big idea.

Transactional – ensures knowledge of goals and how to achieve them.

Transformational – changing, developing and energising people towards greater achievement levels.

Situational – responding to change in situation and context; understanding different needs of people and for leadership.

Dispersed – leadership takes place throughout an organisation or team.

Distributed – empowering members of an organisation or team to take a leading role in areas of interest to them.

Shared – a core of people take decisions following discussion and agreement in the core group.

Invitational – individuals might be invited to lead an initiative that they had come up with.

Collaborative – results from discussion and working together to find a solution to a problem or need and then taking it forward as a democratic team.

Instructional – emanating from the US, one definition concerns monitoring and overseeing teaching in a school in a way that has become familiar in our appraisal climate; the other definition involves head teachers teaching in schools to maintain classroom instruction skills.

Teacher – leading teachers or teachers leading? Perhaps more about teachers taking a lead on a particular professional issue over which they have an interest. Similar to distributed leadership.

Student – connections with pupil voice, but mostly to do with pupils developing initiatives and being given freedom to move their ideas along. Often seen in pupil school councils and representative groups, but can be individually led.

Learning centred – occurs in a 'learning organisation' where all stakeholders are driven by a need to improve learning. Appraisal and inspection are less important in such organisations where there is a 'communal desire to research and find out how learning works'.

(Definitions paraphrased from MacBeath, 2003)

Most of us will probably exhibit a variety of the styles suggested above all at once and many times a day, so it's important to realise that no particular style in the list is recommended as 'best practice'. We must also consider that different events and actions require different styles of leadership, so the truly flexible leader is able to adapt and apply differing techniques where necessary. However, I'm not entirely convinced that it's helpful to refer to these ways of leading as 'styles', as they could be misinterpreted as a style to aspire to. Better, perhaps, to see them as behaviours that we can adopt for a given situation. That said, I'd encourage you to reflect on these definitions and consider how they might resonate with your own practice and experience.

Reflecting on practice

Think of those with whom you work. Can you identify a style of leadership you have observed that has been particularly helpful or inspirational to you?

Do you exhibit a particular leadership style or behaviour yourself?

How versatile or flexible would you say your style or behaviour was?

Would you say that you were weak or strong in a particular style/behaviour?

Distributing leadership

In the study of educational leadership, the concept of 'distributed leadership' is espoused most notably by Gronn (2000) and Spilane (2006). The concept recognises that it is almost impossible to lead a complex organisation like a school in the same way that you would lead troops into battle or a choir in song. The idea of the 'hero leader' in the school context is frankly laughable in most scenarios. The mistake that many teachers, who are new to leadership roles, make is to believe that they can inspire simply by leading from the front: to encourage their team to greatness and to positively affect everything that happens. I've tried – it doesn't always work!

When I first started leading groups of professionals I foolishly believed that they wanted to be led. They didn't. In fact they were quite happy using their own initiative to get on with the job. But I wanted to show them how it was done and to lead by example – the classic 'hero-leader'. How naive! This is fine when your team is inexperienced and needs a role model to follow, but it just doesn't work with most teachers. Understanding this is the first step to being an effective leader in a school and sadly a lesson that a good many senior leaders apparently ignore.

When leading a group of professional teachers it's good to understand that:

- many of them will have experience of doing your job;
- they will have different approaches to achieving your goals;
- they are intelligent and often highly independent people;
- they all have a contribution to make to your project;
- they respond better to praise and recognition than to blame and isolation;
- you need them but they probably don't need you that much.

Naturally, as a leader of anything, you need to have a vision and it's up to you to inspire people to achieve this, but you have to recognise that not everyone will want to follow your path unless they feel part of the decision making process: there needs to be a shared goal.

Distributed leadership recognises that individuals have different strengths and characteristics that contribute to achieving a shared goal. Each colleague in a school has a role to play. By distributing the leadership tasks, individuals are empowered to make decisions and take action without lengthy consultation with senior management. It allows things to progress.

Perhaps of most importance is the concept that leadership is a *dynamic activity*. The relationship between leader and follower in a distributed model is changeable. I can lead one minute, and you the next – I then become the follower. In this way traditional 'roles of authority' may be challenged, and leadership becomes a function of progress rather than a top-down authoritative position with all that that entails.

Example

On a trip to the Yorkshire Dales, one of Jane's pupils became ill. She'd been stung by a wasp and she was reacting badly – her arm was starting to swell and becoming more painful. Sarah and David, two of Jane's team of four, were despatched with the casualty to the nearest hospital A&E department in the school minibus while the rest of the group remained with Jane, the party leader, in the campsite. Mobile phone coverage was poor where they were camped, so when Sarah tried to call to say that the girl needed to be kept in hospital for observation following treatment, she couldn't get through to Jane to pass on the information and agree a next step. Thankfully, each member of staff on the trip had access to parent contact details, pupil medical information and the school's critical incident plan (CIP). David was able to contact the school who contacted the parents, who then travelled to meet them, while Sarah gave the doctors the girl's medical details (including allergies to nuts and penicillin).

In this example the party leader – the person in charge – couldn't exercise leadership because of the distance and poor mobile phone coverage. As leader, it was also her responsibility to stay with the main group and to trust other staff to deal with the girl in question. The protocols and systems that these teachers used were so effective that nobody had to second guess anyone and they knew exactly what to do and how to lead in that situation. You can't call this sort of activity delegation, because nobody told anyone what to do or how to do it. The responsibility of leadership was distributed to Sarah and David, who had the authority to act.

Reflecting on practice

How can you connect with the concept of distributed leadership? Does it challenge you in any way or encourage you to extend your own practice to include it?

Strategic and tactical leadership

If you sit through enough staff meetings and focus groups you'll hear the word 'strategy' used frequently. This kind of thing:

> 'We need to develop a strategy that will take us forward into new ground, and enable focused development via tactical approaches to specific opportunities.'

What does that even mean? Sounds like utter nonsense, doesn't it? Often the people who talk like this don't really understand the difference between strategies and tactics in the first place.

Strategic leadership looks at the big picture. Say, for example, that you want to improve students' independent learning skills. The senior management team has decided that this is a key aspect of the recent OFSTED report the school has just received that needs improvement. Following discussions in staff meetings, it has been decided to make greater use of local museums, galleries and countryside where students can research independent projects on specific subject areas. The educational visits coordinator (EVC) has been put in charge of this and has put together a series of 'good practice' guides, has organised time in the term for the trips and has provided transport and helped to book appropriate resources at designated venues. The EVC has given staff the opportunity to benefit from recent research into school trips and the most effective ways that children can learn in these environments. This is *strategic leadership* from the EVC.

As a teacher in charge of a group of children on one of the subsequent visits, you have decided on a suggested route around the exhibits, meeting places for lunch and roll calls and a buddy-buddy system for looking after one another. You have also allocated colleagues to be available to small groups in the museum. You have set specific learning objectives and have set tasks associated with these. This is *tactical leadership*.

Why not try this?

Tactical or strategic?

Try to identify incidences of your own leadership history that might fit into one of these descriptions. Yet again, however, not all is straightforward as strategy and tactics can overlap from time to time – can you think of examples where this has happened? If so, why?

Leadership 'on the ground' or 'in the field'

Earlier we explored briefly some of what are generally seen as distinct educational leadership styles. Other writers have differing views, of course. In the context of expedition leadership, Langmuir (1995), a good practical thinker and mountain-craft expert, considers a range of leadership 'skills' that he and many others see as essential components of the leadership toolkit for leading expeditions. He suggests that leadership involves:

'Insight

Planning and forethought – anticipation

Checking

Observation

Decision making.'

(Langmuir, 1995)

Langmuir expands on each of the above in his excellent book *Mountaincraft and Leadership*. It's well worth a read even if you never intend to take a party to mountainous country. There's plenty of good advice on a range of issues including weather and first aid.

Mountain leadership syllabuses will contain a set of competences similar to these that must be achieved in order to pass a course such as the Mountain Leader (Summer/Winter) course run by the National Mountain Centre in Plas-y-Brenin in North Wales. So rather than a rigidly defined collection of styles that we can pigeon-hole leaders into, we have a menu or a recommended toolkit with which leaders can work. At any given time there is a 'best fit' solution or way of behaving and that reacts to a situation or context.

One of our great assets as teachers is that we have many different roles to perform during a day, be it form tutor, class teacher, lunch supervisor or colleague observer. We flit from one role to the other and are flexible in the way we react to different situations. This leadership behaviour is vital when on school trips as the situations and norms can be so vastly different from what we are used to. Without being flexible and reactive, we'd surely fail. Perhaps we should ask Langmuir to add 'versatility' to his list.

Reflecting on practice

Part 2 of this book will discuss a range of scenarios and dilemmas in some detail. But in this last chapter in Part 1, it's worth thinking about your own trips and where you've had to react to a changing situation or change plans in the middle of a trip.

How did you handle the challenge?

What behaviours did you exhibit?

How not to lead

This should be the easiest aspect of leadership to think about. We've all seen appalling examples of leadership during our careers and we can critically reflect on other people's practice, but rarely do we reflect on our own in the same way. Having very established ideas about methods of leading school trips can lead to problems, and fundamentally misjudging your audience and your role on such a trip can have an alienating effect on your pupils and actually discourage them from the type of learning that you are hoping to foster.

Keeping in mind the notion of drawing on your leadership toolkit in response to contexts and situations as they change and evolve, here are two scenarios that raise questions about the organisation of the trip, quality of the leadership and even the rationale for the trip in the first place. The first is a snapshot summary of a trip to a museum and the second is an observation from an overseas trip.

Case study

Leadership example 1

Setting: A large museum in a city centre

Age range: 9–10 (boys and girls)

How many people? 30 pupils, three staff and a museum guide

Picture the scene: Pupils were being led around the museum by a member of the museum staff who had been attempting to explain a small number of key principles using examples in the museum's collection. The museum guide had an unfortunate habit of repeating a key phrase over and over and spoke softly and in a monotone voice. School staff were present, along with chaperones, and pupils behaved well generally but were amused when the key phrase kept being repeated – they started to giggle more as the tour went on. The guided part of the tour was completed and pupils were given free time to carry out an investigation of the manufacturing materials collection which was displayed in a large area with a range of activities, touch-screen terminals and imaginatively arranged exhibits with large pieces of flexible plastic hanging down from the ceiling to the floor.

When the pupils were released from the guided tour they were told to get on with their investigations by the lead teacher. No other words of assistance or advice were given. The pupils dispersed in all directions and the teachers spoke briefly to the guide before heading for the café where they had lunch.

What went wrong? Few pupils appeared to get on well with the task despite the well-prepared worksheet that asked good questions and allowed pupils to choose independently what they wanted to investigate. Some pupils started to use the interactive touch-screen terminals, while others found a quiet place to sit and chat, with worksheets left on the ground. About ten of the pupils ran among hanging plastic sheeting, playing hide and seek and generally creating a good deal of noise. Those pupils who had started with the exhibits either joined in or sat down and went through the worksheets without properly looking through the exhibit. After a short while, most had found a spot to sit and eat a packed lunch that they all had in their backpacks.

Reflecting on practice

Any of this sound familiar?

How would you have done things differently?

How could you have improved the investigation element at the time?

How could you work with venue staff to ensure success?

Think of three simple and specific tactical measures that might have avoided some of the problems, while maintaining the focus of the trip.

Key reflections

This is an example of a trip that could have gone extremely well. The museum was well resourced, with free facilities and expertise that gave the pupils superb access to information and activity in equal amount. The museum also provided an optional workshop facility where pupils could have been guided through a discovery activity. The school chose to use its own excellent worksheets, though, and this was fine as it was clear that the author had visited the museum in order to write them. However, more thought could have been given to the following areas.

Collaboration and communication

It was clear that the author of the worksheets was not the same person as the organiser of the trip, as she showed no interest in the sheets when instructing the pupils to get on with their investigations. Having said that, the trip was well organised in terms of logistics, staffing and activities; everyone knew where to go and what time to be there, it's just a shame that the teaching staff chose to have lunch during the most important part of the trip.

A need for practical leadership on the ground

Behaviour, learning objectives and tactical issues were given scant regard in the planning and the only leadership observed was leading the teaching staff away from the pupils. The museum guide was knowledgeable but needed help and reassurance from the teachers. It would have helped him if one of the teachers had mentioned his habit of repeating a key phrase. This may have lightened the atmosphere a little too.

Timings and structure

Was it necessary to have a tour before the investigation activity, as it turned out that the two were not connected? The tour related to some previous work that the class had done, while the investigation concerned a future topic. Would it have been better to get the pupils to do their investigation before lunch when they could be supervised and guided by their teachers, and then do a tour after a proper lunch break? By being absent from the most useful aspect of the trip the teachers missed an opportunity to really engage with the learning that their pupils were doing.

Activity planning and learning objectives

This is definitely an example of a trip where planning has been an inconsistent aspect of the endeavour. This is a common failing of school trips, where all the logistical organisational aspects are very well done but the actual activities that the pupils engage in end up being less than satisfactory. The trip is rushed and the outcome merely achieves a day away from school. In terms of achieving learning objectives or adding to classroom learning, this sort of trip misses the mark.

Resist the temptation to do too much
It may have been better to make things much simpler. Trying to do too much can often lead to an outcome like the one described above. When using well-resourced museums and galleries it is tempting to try to do everything, but as discussed in Chapter 2 it's often better to set even fewer objectives than you might set in a 30-minute lesson. Allowing pupils to immerse themselves in a simpler activity might enable them to do it properly and reflect on their learning.

Case study

Leadership example 2

Setting: Overseas adventurous activity trip

Age range: 11–14 (boys)

How many? 30 pupils and five staff

Picture the scene: This trip took place in a mainland European country at a ski resort. A party of boys had been at the resort for two days and were having two hour lessons in the morning and two in the afternoon. These lessons were separated by a two-hour lunch break, when ski instructors either had time off or continued teaching other lessons. Lunch was provided in a self-service canteen which also served other school groups and the general public. At lunchtimes the place was at bursting point and canteen staff were keen to get those who had finished to leave. The net result was around 150–200 boys and girls milling around outside the canteen for most of the two-hour period waiting for their lessons to start. On this occasion the school's staff were late into lunch and stayed during most of the two hours, having earlier been rushing around trying to fix a problem with one of their pupils' kit. The staff were all competent skiers, but travelled as one group for most of the morning so where the leader went the rest followed.

What went wrong? Very quickly, and with no apparent warning, two of the older boys in the group started to fight, causing passers-by to ski around them and take avoiding action. What could have appeared to be harmless rough and tumble soon turned nasty when one of the boys started to kick the other in the stomach while wearing heavy plastic ski boots. A passing member of staff from another school intervened, separated the two boys and sent for their teacher. Luckily neither boy was badly injured and their teacher took good control of the situation and applied appropriate sanctions there and then.

Reflecting on practice

Have you ever dealt with a similar situation?

What is an appropriate amount of unsupervised free time for pupils?

How does context make a difference?

What sanctions would you apply to the two boys concerned?

Key reflections

This was an unfortunate incident and the blame cannot be laid firmly at anyone's door in particular. Nevertheless, the following factors combined to cause a scenario that made the incident more likely.

The amount of unsupervised free time

Two hours is a long time to wait and boys can get bored very easily. There is nothing wrong with leaving pupils of secondary school age to their own devices for a little while, but you'd need to have a checking in protocol, or delegate responsibility to a senior pupil to help maintain order. The trip's 'specific risk assessment' should have considered unsupervised time.

The lack of time for lunch and the rushed atmosphere

Just like the rest of us, children hate being pushed around and rushed, particularly at mealtimes when they might want to rest after the physical exertions of a morning's activity. Being rushed is annoying and so causes resentment.

Pupil relationship history

Clearly there was an existing problem in the relationship between the two boys as the incident flared up so quickly. An awareness of your pupils' complex relationships with each other is essential on school trips. Separating the two boys to start with or even just keeping a close eye on them would have gone some way to easing tensions. Nevertheless, if children are determined to wind each other up, they'll find a way no matter what you do. All you can do in such circumstances is your best. Contacting tutors before the trip could have uncovered previous problems between pupils.

Staff travelling as a group

By sticking together for most of the time as a whole staff group, the ability to observe and check up on your charges is diminished. Had the staff group been split into two or three groups, they could have been on time for lunch, leaving two to sort out the equipment problem. This may have enabled the staff to tour round the group after the pupils had finished lunch and check on progress in the morning and on general wellbeing. Any issues of conflict could have been spotted by the experienced teachers and dealt with or subdued. A set of well-designed protocols for dealing with behaviour and supervising could have helped too, enabling the staff to act appropriately.

Local knowledge

Had pupils been able to return to their hotel for lunch and some rest, things might have been different. An extended period of waiting could have proved a bigger problem if the weather had deteriorated as it often does in the mountains. This is where local knowledge is so important. Travel companies and travel representatives are notorious for giving only basic information about a destination and its facilities. You can combat this by going on an inspection trip if one is offered, asking difficult questions, expecting good answers and insisting on seeing what you need to see. Developing some local knowledge can really help move your trip along in the right direction.

Easy mistakes to make, just as easy to avoid

The teachers involved in both of these trips were professional, caring and responsible people who worked hard on many aspects of the trip. However, most of the problems were caused or exacerbated by inadequate planning or tactical leadership and were centred around unsupervised time. Let's not forget that leadership is not the sole responsibility of the designated leader or organiser. In both cases a distributed model of leadership might have improved matters, giving individuals the opportunity to plan for different aspects of the trip and take a lead in ensuring that they were appropriately dealt with.

Collaborative planning is the way forward here, enabling ideas and questions to be bounced around. Giving everyone involved a chance to contribute can throw up some unexpected concerns or useful suggestions and can help to avoid problematic issues. Later in this chapter there is an exploration of the use of protocols for dealing with routine situations and unexpected problems, and these are best designed collaboratively well before your trip takes place.

Thorough planning helps to keep colleagues well informed, decide on objectives and set success criteria. In this way your team will share a common goal and this can only add to a positive approach to your trip.

Being positive

Earlier I suggested that no specific leadership style is suitable for continual use. We dip in and out of styles of behaviour, picking them from our toolkit as needed. In this section I want to explore briefly the notion that leading on school trips needs to be done from a positive standpoint – something that I'm sure we'd all agree on, but also worth thinking about why. Trying to inspire through negative behaviours and motivations does little to help young people learn, or make colleagues want to work with you. Nevertheless, being sarcastic and apportioning blame are types of behaviour that are all too easy to slip into. Being inconsistent in your approach to people and problems won't help either, as Paul Dix explains:

> *'Being consistent in dealing with the behaviour of your students means that they know what will happen if they choose to break the rules and equally they know what will happen if they choose to follow the rules.'*

> (Dix, 2007: 17)

You need to remain consistent and authoritative, yet positive and approachable:

> *'Teachers who are firm but fair and have a sense of humour are those most likely to win the hearts and minds of pupils.'*

> (Davies, 2006: 137)

I'm fairly confident that we'd all agree that learning is an emotional activity. A positive frame of mind with encouraging stimulation seems to have a greater effect on learners' retention of knowledge and development of skill than negative stimuli. That is not to say that we don't all remember an occasion where we learned not to do something as a result of a negative experience, like the pain caused by touching a hot plate, for example.

The right motivations

Praise and recognition, respect and reciprocity, and encouragement and trust are words that conjure up memories of good feelings and the creation of self-worth and self-efficacy – you are a valuable member of the group and you have something to contribute; you develop social capital in yourself and others. Surely all of this seems self-evident, so why do we still see teachers, senior leaders and parents using negative stimuli with children?

For me, it comes down to what you are trying to achieve through your trip or activity – what are your motives? By examining your reasons for engaging in the trip through some careful self-reflection, you might identify some good and some questionable practice, or positive and negative aspects of your leadership. There's nothing wrong with identifying negative aspects of your own practice, as long as you try to fix them.

I understand that it is extremely difficult to remain positive when you're sat waiting for a group to check in on an expedition, and it's raining, or you've just cleared up the third pile of vomit on a long coach journey. But there are positive ways of looking at this sort of occurrence, as there are too when children misbehave. Children and young adults really do learn by making mistakes, and it is helping them to realise this that can be most rewarding at times. Positives can emerge from negatives.

Maintaining a productive atmosphere

Let's be honest, some teachers really do love the sound of their own voice; it's a sad fact but they do exist. Some even appear to achieve efficacy by proving to their pupils that they know more than they do. I'm sure I'm not the only teacher to have observed lessons where the level of self-promotion on the part of the teacher is almost embarrassing. Here the only positive effect is felt by the teacher who is boosting their ego because they have a stage on which to perform and a captive audience.

When pupils mess around on a field trip or in the classroom the first course of action for some is to seek to blame and point out what the pupil has done wrong:

> If you'd done what I said and listened to me, you wouldn't be in this situation. You don't listen, do you! You just do your own thing and ignore the conse-quences and everyone else.

All this achieves is to make the pupil feel worse and the teacher feel a range of emotions from power to disappointment. The pupil is forced to reflect on the negative aspects of their behaviour or performance. We see this often in poorly judged sports coaching comment, and the coaches wonder why their half-time 'ear-bashing' fails to have effect. The entrenching of the notion, often held among pupils, that the pupil/teacher relationship is a 'them and us' kind, is extremely unhelpful especially on a school trip. This kind of comment to a pupil breeds resentment:

> You're being stupid, you were told to bring strong footwear and you've ignored the advice. How can you hope to get on at A-level if you can't follow simple orders?

The pupil in question here was wearing training shoes in a wet mountainous area and was part of another school group I observed when walking with my own party of teenagers. Although most certainly in the wrong, this sort of comment did nothing for the pupil's self-esteem, ignored possible family economic reasons for her lack of appropriate footwear and may have damaged her performance in the exercise they were carrying out.

During a field trip, pupils are in an unfamiliar environment where nerves and uncertainty may play a part in their behaviour. School trips are special occasions for many pupils and there is a great deal of excitement and anticipation surrounding them. Pupils look forward to something different and some have trouble adjusting their behaviour to new and unusual social settings. The pupil involved in the comment above was fairly resilient, but a more sensitive pupil might, quite rightly, have been upset and 'knocked back' by the suggestion that she might be no good at A-level and lowered her expectations further. Being away from home adds to the impact of negative comments where the usual support network of family is not available to work through such issues. Social capital can actually be damaged.

You have a dual role – you are authority and carer

As leader you set the tone. Pupils may be away from home for several days and you need to establish a number of things before you go and when you get there. One thing you could do that might well have a positive effect on their learning as well as their self-esteem, while also improving your relationship with them, is to use a questioning style of interaction. This requires you to ask questions to establish feelings, thoughts, knowledge, opinions and facts. There are some occasions that warrant a severe telling off, but most cases can be dealt with more discreetly and achieve a desired and more comfortable outcome. To give an example, I've rephrased the examples I used a little earlier:

From this:

> If you'd done what I said and listened to me, you wouldn't be in this situation. You don't listen, do you! You just do your own thing and ignore the consequences and everyone else.

To this:

> I wish you'd paid attention to my concerns before. We're in a situation now that we need to resolve. How are we going to do that?

And from this:

> You're being stupid, you were told to bring strong footwear and you've ignored the advice. How can you hope to get on at A-level if you can't follow simple orders?

To this:

I asked everyone to bring strong footwear and you're wearing trainers. They're not as safe as boots so you risk injury. Is there a reason you weren't able to do what I asked? How are we going to resolve this? What's the best way forward?

Note that in both examples I've tried to suggest that solving the problem can be done together and I've not related the current problem to future academic progress or called the pupil's general intelligence into question. I've also identified a number of facts about the incident and then tried to establish whether they are acceptable to the pupil. This gives the pupil an opportunity to reflect positively rather than dwell on what they've done leading up to the meeting. To break this down into easy steps might be more helpful:

- Present the known facts.
- Establish what is acceptable.
- Ask how the situation can be resolved together.

It might sound a little trite and 'fluffy', but being positive in your leadership approach can present *problems* as *opportunities* for change and improvement. For me, this whole approach has had a huge impact on the way I work and how I view challenges. By reframing battles with difficult people into opportunities, you get to the end of the day with a lighter load and a better feeling about your effectiveness. That said, there are no quick and easy answers to some problems, and with most things there is an appropriate behaviour for each different situation. Nevertheless, a generally positive approach from you as the leader might negate some problems ever existing, particularly those that result from difficult relationships between some staff and their pupils.

> **Why not try this?**
>
> We've all dealt with things badly in the past. Try to recall a situation that you weren't happy with, either on a trip or at school. Work through it again and try to imagine how you could have managed it differently — more positively perhaps.

Freedom or control?

How much control do you want or need to have? How much freedom do your pupils need or desire?

Control and freedom are not mutually exclusive concepts. It is possible to have a high level of control yet give the impression of freedom to your pupils. Of course, pupils of different ages will need to be controlled in different ways, but please don't misunderstand me. I'm not talking about control in the sense that we manipulate the pupils or control how they think; rather control in this context refers to your management of a group of individuals in a way that helps them safely achieve their individual learning objectives. Most children love the freedom to explore and investigate the world around them, and young children are used to this sort of activity through play. But there is only so far you can get by adopting this approach: some structure for control is needed.

During a visit to a science museum, say, you might be focused on exploring electricity. Your pupils will be *controlled* to visit the exhibits and interactive stands in order to achieve this – you're likely to have a route to follow and a suggestion of what exhibits to look at first in order to guide the pupils through the learning path that you've developed. The pupils have an element of freedom to learn while moving around and talking freely – a very different and welcome change to sitting at a desk in a classroom. This is great: sounds like you've thought of everything and have taken account of timings and what can be achieved on the day. But what if something more interesting (for the pupils) catches their eye? A child rushes up to you with great excitement and wants to explore something she's just seen or heard about that isn't on the list. Do you insist that she gets on with your chosen tasks and suggest that she comes back, or do you build on her enthusiasm by thinking on your feet and changing plans? Not only do you have to give sufficient control and freedom to the visit, but you also need to recognise when to adapt and reassess.

TOP TIP!

Build a level of freedom into your learning activities. Allow some choice in what the children can do.

When away from school you should always have one eye on child safety issues. I sometimes hear from teachers that a school trip is a success when everyone gets off the bus at the end of the day still with all their fingers and toes and smiles on their faces – a bit flippant and meant in jest, but this attitude isn't good enough. You can't control your pupils' every move, but there will be times when you need to have everyone in view or stuck together so you can all get on a train, or stay safe in a big crowd, or cross a busy road.

However, you must be prepared to allow control to be an elastic concept. You can't put your pupils in a bubble. You can be in control, able to react and respond to issues and problems, able to gather your group together and ensure their safety, without being restrictive.

> **TOP TIP!**
>
> *Have a supervision or group control plan (see the protocol in Figure 4.1). Agree on times and places to meet and what you are going to do when an activity finishes or you have a break. What will you do with the pupils?*

Being in control of large groups of children relies on systems and good communication – in the same way 150 police officers can control 30,000 football fans on a regular basis. The officer in charge has good information and communication from their officers and has systems in place to avoid trouble. So your team is an essential component of your trip – make sure they know what you expect and that there is agreement about the way forward, but try to remember that one of the key aspects of leading intelligent and resourceful professionals is not to talk down to them.

Four systems for managing freedom/control

In some circumstances you'll hand over the control and safety of your group to an instructor or a guide, say during the day on an outward bound trip. In others you'll need to manage things yourself, say on the way to a museum from the station or during a data collection exercise during a field trip. In both cases you need to develop an overall strategy and tactics for specific challenges. The four systems, or layers, of control suggested below might help you consider your options.

High profile control – staff led
When you are out with a group of pupils the staff will always be in direct control. You'll do a roll call at regular intervals, when you think it is needed, and ensure that as the leader of the trip you are highly visible to your pupils and the general public. This is a really effective method when you have a small or younger group, but can cause problems with older pupils and larger groups (of more than 20): you risk communication and attention problems. Everything will take more time, even though you'll be communicating to one large group it's likely that not everyone will hear or pay attention. A better approach is to lower your apparent level of control by delegating headcounts and information to your staff team.

Low profile control – staff/senior pupil led
With groups over 20 this is my preferred method, especially in public places such as airports, museums and galleries. Low profile control allows a more relaxed atmosphere to penetrate your trip. You'll have an appropriate ratio of staff to pupils and you should assign small groups of pupils to a group leader, and at

various stages in your trip you can ask the group leaders to confirm they've got everyone.

If you have a range of ages that include senior pupils, say sixth formers, you can use these pupils to help control the group. Small groups are best either organised by year, form or house. Give each group leader a list and keep all groups to the same number to make it easier to count. When you get to your bus or to the boarding gate at the airport you can just go round your leaders and quietly check up on who's where.

The buddy-buddy system

This is another excellent low profile group control method and encourages pupils to take responsibility for each other. However, it can only be used effectively with older pupils (year 6 and above in certain circumstances – your call) and in conjunction with another layer of checks, as if it both 'buddies' are missing it's no good asking if everyone's buddy is present. Nevertheless, when you set your group off on a study of an exhibit, the buddy-buddy system is invaluable not only in ensuring care and safety but also in providing a 'study-buddy'.

Remote supervision

Duke of Edinburgh's Award expeditions immediately spring to mind as an example of where remote supervision is appropriate. The best thing to do here is to encourage the buddy-buddy system within each group, but to shadow the group or check in at regular intervals (how often depends on the age of the group and the nature of the environment). If you can travel by car or minibus between checkpoints with a colleague, you can also walk to meet up with a number of different groups by intercepting them along their routes.

> **Reflecting on practice**
>
> What's the best system to use for your pupils and your type of trip?
>
> Which would be best for:
> - A year 4 visit to a zoo?
> - A year 9 geography field trip?
> - A mixed age scuba diving trip to Egypt?

Practical leadership – who's in charge here?

Not a bad question to ask actually. Would it be obvious to an onlooker that you are in charge of your group? Can any member of your staff team deal with any situation?

During a ski trip to Italy recently, one of our local Italian instructors lost one of our beginners from her group. Rather than phone in to report this, she carried on until lunchtime when we finally heard the news. We only located the girl when an American gentleman who'd found her at a chairlift looking confused and lost took control, left her with his wife and family at a café and went looking for her teachers. By chance, he approached my colleague and asked whether we were looking for a lost pupil – we were just standing in a lift queue, discussing the piste map and making plans to organise a search. I imagine that our bearing, conversation, body language, large rucksacks and radios must have given the game away. But still, our new American friend had an idea of the sort of people who might be in charge of a group of kids on the slopes.

I'm not suggesting that you swagger around looking as though you own the place, but you should try to give an impression of confidence and purpose to your pupils and those in your general vicinity. Here are some suggestions:

- Look as though you know what you are doing and what you expect to happen next.
- Be calm and approachable.
- Don't ruin everyone's day by marching up and down barking orders at people.
- Lead, don't dictate.

Confidence to deal with problems

Being confident gives your pupils and staff team the reassurance that they are in good hands and allows them to get on with the trip. Your confidence will also spill over to the general public and to helpers or instructors who are part of your trip or visit. Further, you need to ensure that you are confident enough to deal with the difficult problems that occasionally crop up during a visit – when the question of 'Who's in charge here?' is really important.

Let's say a member of the museum staff or the public has a complaint to make about one of your pupils. Most often they'll want to talk to whoever has the greatest power to provide some sort of solution to the problem, and that's you! Whatever the problem might be, you'll need to act decisively and give others the confidence that you are doing the right thing. Of course, you might not be dealing with a disciplinary issue; you could be dealing with a lost pupil, a case of theft or assault on one of your party, or even a dispute on the football pitch during an away match. Whatever it is you'll need to draw on your experience and resources to calm the waters and make the necessary arrangements to deal with the problem. You're in charge – people will listen to you and respect your opinion.

Often though, the right way to deal with a problem will spring to mind after the event, so it's important to have an idea of how you might react to some problems before you encounter them. Here are some tips for dealing with problems:

- Never act immediately unless people are in peril.
- Establish the facts.
- Be calm and reassuring.
- Don't accuse or take sides.
- Be serious and professional with all.
- Smile and maintain eye contact when talking and listening.
- Avoid sarcasm.
- Listen to all and try not to interrupt until a person has finished speaking.

Don't forget that when you're away from school your support network is diminished and you can't call on help and advice as easily or as immediately, so anything positive that you can do to deal with situations as they arise will help bring them to a successful conclusion.

Reflecting on practice

Dealing with complaints is a challenging area. You have to be fair and be seen to do your job. But what if, following your investigations, you find no wrongdoing? Do you have the confidence to be an advocate for those in your care, not just their judge?

How would you communicate your decision? Don't forget the advice above about being positive.

What about recording and reporting your findings – do you have a system?

Protocols for distributing practical leadership

Protocols are extremely useful tools for any organisation. Along with a healthy dose of initiative and grit, they are the bread and butter of emergency service organisations who deal with problems on a daily basis. In simple terms, protocols provide structure and ways forward for particular situations. They rely on a mechanical style response to a given input (if X happens, do Y in response).

In schools we use protocols for a range of situations, from registering in the morning to dealing with behavioural issues in lessons, and I've already alluded to their effectiveness in earlier chapters of this book. In all cases where protocols are used, a situation or scenario has been considered and a system designed to control it. For our purposes there are two types of protocol that are useful to discuss:

Routine protocols – where the type of scenario is expected, happens often and requires some control or organisation (e.g. pupil illness in class).

Auxiliary protocols – where an unexpected, but planned for, scenario occurs and requires an immediate and controlled response (e.g. a flu outbreak or flooding).

Meeting colleagues for planning sessions often produces 'What are we going to do if...?' questions that may not have previously been thought of by the party leader. This is an opportunity to design a protocol, or redesign an existing one. The best protocols are the ones that become second nature, and on a school trip they negate the need for time-consuming consultation. If everyone knows what needs to happen for a given situation, there is no need to talk about it, so team members can exercise distributed leadership and get on with the job. I think this is what people mean when they report back after a trip and say things like 'It ran like a well-oiled machine' or 'We all worked well together because we deal with things in the same way'. Teachers on these trips don't need to second-guess each other as they know how they will react. That's often the result of years of working together, but for new teachers a protocol is an effective substitute for a long collegial working relationship.

Such protocols can help with dilemmas such as: what to do about alcohol abuse on a trip; what to do if a child is sick on a coach journey; how to deal with behaviour issues; how to deal with problem staff; what to do when a pupil needs to go to hospital, and so on. Part of the value in designing protocols is in the activity of sitting down with colleagues and thinking really hard about the trip ahead.

Critical incident plan (CIP)

Sadly, many schools rely on a generic critical incident plan (CIP) protocol for dealing with unexpected emergencies, and some might simply say 'If something goes wrong we have a CIP and we follow that.' While some CIPs can be very well written, they can lack an understanding of practical situations and be too generic. Often, teachers are unaware of the contents of their own CIP and rely on common sense alone. A well-written and useful CIP would be produced in consultation with teachers who actually run school trips. This would produce a useful document that is firmly rooted in practical experience.

Below are two protocols for different situations. One is a regular occurrence, so the protocol is routine. The other is for an unexpected occurrence so is auxiliary.

Protocol example 1

This is a really simple protocol for moving around a busy city centre (see Figure 4.1). In the context of school trips it's a **routine protocol** as you'd use it often, but you might never have seen it written down as it's mostly common sense. Nevertheless, you can't rely on everyone to possess the same level of common sense as you. Don't worry, there is no suggestion here that you need to write everything down if you want to call it a protocol. It's just helpful to illustrate the idea.

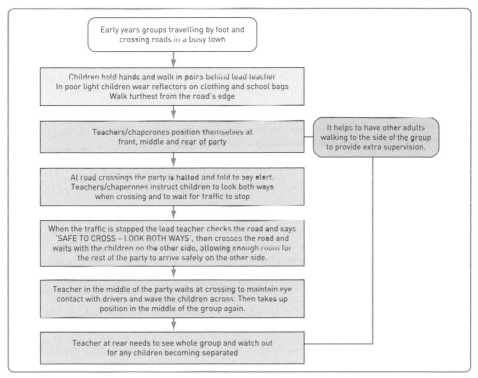

Fig 4.1: Routine protocol for travelling by foot with early years pupils

Protocol example 2

This protocol (Figure 4.2) is a little more detailed and was designed to deal with a serious accident or illness while on an activity trip, so it's an **auxiliary protocol**. Thankfully these types of protocol are rarely put into action, but despite all our efforts to avoid serious problems, if one were to occur we would all hope to be able to deal with it as professionally as possible. This example is by no means perfect, but it illustrates one way that colleagues have thought through an activity well in advance.

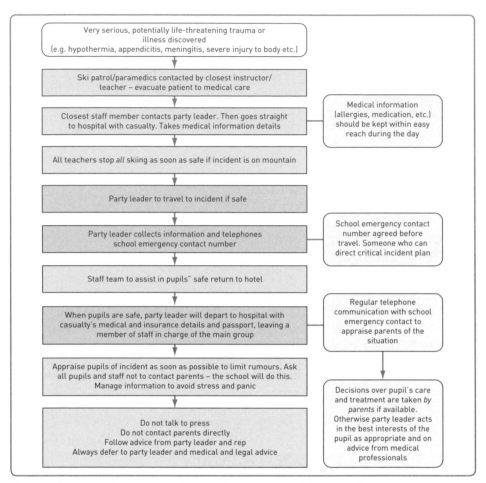

Fig 4.2: dealing with a serious injury or illness on an activity style trip

As a school trip party leader, having a well-rehearsed set of protocols is hugely reassuring. Knowing that everyone around you can react to situations as they arise in a manner that removes doubt and indecisiveness, and give you the support you need to ensure the right outcome, is priceless. Designing protocols needn't be time consuming, but you do need to sit down and start asking the 'What if...?' questions long before you leave for your trip.

Conclusion

So much of what we know about leadership comes from our everyday dealings with people in a wide range of contexts. Something not yet referred to is the concept of having 'people skills'. For me, these, mixed with a good dollop of common sense, make for an excellent base from which to start leading, or teaching for that matter. The important aspects of your trip, such as achieving the agreed goals and objectives, enjoying the activity, actively engaging in learning, being responsible and being safe, need to be achieved in a spirit of harmony, teamwork and with a sense of shared purpose. None of this is possible if the person making key decisions and taking a lead can't get on with others.

As well as giving due concern to the strategies, techniques, tactics and approaches to leading a school trip, you need to approach the people involved with care and kindness along the way. Including the people involved in a trip (pupils and staff) in the planning process is a way of achieving shared ownership and more sustainable outcomes. Don't forget that you and your staff team can learn on field trips too. You can learn about each other's practice, the subject matter of the trip, managing groups of children, leading adult professionals, planning and organisation, and dealing with dilemmas.

In the next part of this book you will read about a range of interesting and challenging dilemmas that other education professionals have faced and dealt with. You will have to decide how you would deal with the dilemmas before you read how the leader at the time arrived at their solution. The examples are taken from real events and changed only slightly to protect identities and locations.

Key ideas summary

- School trips offer a chance for you to develop real leadership skills and experience.
- Leadership is a dynamic activity that requires versatility.
- What works in the classroom might not work outside it.
- Planning needs to be strategic and tactical. Think carefully about aims and objectives.
- Be positive – remember the human touch too.
- Decide on the level of freedom and control that you'll need.
- Be confident in your leadership.
- Develop protocols with your colleagues.
- Encourage distributed leadership.

Going further

Websites

For emergencies and critical incident plans (CIPs):

www.teachernet.gov.uk/emergencies

For all government documents concerning school trips:

www.teachernet.gov.uk/docbank

For educational leadership:

www.leadershipforlearning.org.uk

www.nationalcollege.org.uk

For outdoor leadership:

www.mltuk.org

www.pyb.co.uk

www.snowsportengland.org.uk

www.lotc.org.uk

Further reading

Davies, S. (2006) *The Essential Guide to Teaching* (Harlow: Pearson).

DfES (2005) *Leading and Coordinating CPD in Secondary Schools* (Nottingham: DfES).

DfES (2002) *Handbook for Group Leaders* (Nottingham: DfES).

DfES (2002) *Standards for Adventure Part 2* (Nottingham: DfES).

DfES (1998) *Health and Safety of Pupils on Educational Visits* (Nottingham: DfES).

Dix,P. (2007) *Taking Care of Behaviour* (Harlow: Pearson).

Fullan, M. (2003) *The Moral Imperative of School Leadership* (Thousand Oaks, CA: Corwin Press).

Jackson, B. and Parry, K. (2008) *A Very Short, Fairly Interesting and Reasonably Cheap Book About Studying Leadership* (London: Sage).

Keay, W. (2000) *Expedition Guide* (Wellingborough: Sterling Press).

Langmuir, E. (1995) *Mountaincraft and Leadership* (Edinburgh: Scottish Sports Council).

→

MacBeath, J. (2008) Not so much a passion more a way of life. In Davies, B. and Brighouse, T. (eds), *Passionate Leadership in Education* (London: Sage).

MacBeath, J. (2003) The Alphabet Soup of Leadership, *Inform,* Jan 2003 (2).

Spilane, J. (2006) *Distributed Leadership* (San Francisco, CA: Jossey-Bass).

West-Burnham, J. and O'Sullivan, F. (1998) *Leadership and Professional Development in Schools: How to promote techniques for effective professional learning* (London: Financial Times Professional).

Relevant research studies

Darling-Hammond, L. and McLaughlin, M. (1996) Policies that Support Professional Development in an Era of Reform. In McLaughlin, M. and Oberman, I. (eds), *Teacher Learning: New policies, new practices* (New York: Teachers College Press).

Frost, D. (2006) The Concept of 'Agency' in Leadership for Learning, *Leading and Managing*, 12 (2), 19–28.

Gronn, P. (2000) Distributed Properties: A new architecture for leadership, *Educational Management and Administration*, 28 (3), 317–338.

Hindin, A., Morocco, C., Mott, E. and Aguilar, C. (2007) More Than Just a Group: Teacher collaboration and learning in the workplace, *Teachers and Teaching: Theory and Practice*, 13 (4), 349–376.

Kendell, S., Murfield, J., Dillon, J. and Wilkin, A. (2006) *Education Outside the Classroom: Research to identify what training is offered by initial teacher training institutions* (Research Report 802) (Nottingham: DfES).

OFSTED (2008) *Geography in Schools: Changing practice* (London: OFSTED).

Pedder, D., Storey, A. and Opfer, V. (2008) *Schools and Continuing Professional Development (CPD) in England – State of the Nation research project* (London: TDA).

Turner, C. (2006) Subject Leaders in Secondary Schools and Informal Learning: Towards a conceptual framework, *School Leadership and Management*, 26 (5), 419–435.

Trant, J. (2009) *To What Extent do Teachers View School Fieldtrips as Opportunities for Their Own Learning?* MEd. Thesis (Faculty of Education, University of Cambridge).

Before you move on to the next part …

Read through these general hints and tips for running a good trip.

Experience is a great and wonderful thing, allowing you to view situations through a sharper lens at times, but clouding your vision through tradition at others. The experience of others can help you shape your methods and opinions of what is right to do in any situation. This advice has been gathered from suitably experienced colleagues and may be a helpful way of summarising what you've just read.

Planning

- Get everything down on paper – a paper trail is essential in today's world. All of your decisions and permissions must be absolutely watertight.
- Visit your destination and write your risk assessment collaboratively.
- Know your school policies and follow them to the letter – if you ever stray from these you'll get little sympathy if things go wrong.
- Communication must be first rate. Dates, meeting points, departure times, modes of travel, trip objectives, costs and an itinerary must be available early on and to everyone (pupils, parents, staff, EVC, head teacher and so on).
- Know your escape routes, nearest hospitals and back-up travel plans.
- Arrange for a contingency fund to be available should you need emergency items – these can range from new clothing in case of a sudden rain shower to ambulances or medical costs if things get bad.
- Organise your staff/helpers before you go – who's going to do what? Get this done very early on and involve them in the planning process.

Getting there

- Make sure you have set out what is acceptable behaviour on your journey.
- Explain the itinerary.
- Let everyone know what you want them to do if there is a problem.
- Use your staff effectively – communicate the plan to them and allow them to disseminate information to your pupils as and when.

● If using a private-hire coach, make sure someone is appointed to do a 'sweep' of it before you get off each time.

At your destination

● Reinforce acceptable behaviour boundaries, bedtimes, alcohol and smoking policies and fire procedures if you're staying overnight. Discuss local laws and customs if you're staying overseas.
● Organise regular meeting points and times for roll calls.
● Keep learning activities focused and to a timetable.
● Allow free time for pupils to talk about their work or just to socialise
● Spend as much time as you can interacting with your pupils.

When you're out there: reacting to challenges

Introduction

When we actually get 'out there' with the children it's almost possible to forget the many weeks or months of planning that have gone into a trip. Interacting with the children and helping them to find their feet as learners is what we signed up for – the cut and thrust of dealing with the demands of busy young minds is exciting and life-affirming when things go well. We all have off days, of course, but on the whole the job of a teacher is pretty dynamic and enjoyable, I think.

With school trips and educational visits, the important part for the children is the visit itself, the activity or just being away from school. But for you it's the planning that must take priority; you can't go out there and just 'wing it' – that's tempting fate!

Even if you've planned to the very last detail and followed all the advice in this book, you'll find something that needs to be addressed that you hadn't thought of. It's the nature of people that there are many possible outcomes for any given situation depending on how we feel and how we interact with and respond to each other. Each person brings a different history and experience and all types of baggage with them to each and every situation.

The situations that people find themselves in are influenced by the places in which they happen and the other people around them. We see this all the time in schools with different behaviours among children. A child might be terribly behaved in one classroom with one set of classmates and teacher, but delightful in another room with a different set and different teacher. It's the 'Well, he's always very well behaved for me' scenario that you hear so often in school staffrooms.

On school trips, challenges tend to be magnified because of the separation from the school's support network and regular systems for managing behaviour, illness and injury, for example. As has already been mentioned, you can't pass the problems up the line when you're away from school – you have to deal with them then and there, and speedily.

Part 2 focuses on challenges and problems that colleagues have faced over recent years when leading and helping to lead school trips. There are a good range of pupil ages, staff experience and types of school represented in the stories that follow, so identifying with the people behind them should be straightforward. Each chapter deals with issues that you may well be faced with at some point. They are neither trivial nor hopelessly difficult challenges, just real stories that I have come across during my research that might resonate with your own experiences. They boil down to dealing with people and the places and situations in which they find themselves and the challenges that emerge.

Throughout Part 2, as in Part 1, you'll find opportunities to stop and reflect on the stories, and to consider your own course of action. There are many other challenging scenarios in the Appendix that you can consider, but the stories that follow have been analysed and dissected in order to highlight relevant educational, leadership or child safety issues.

Challenges when working with children and adults on school trips

What this chapter will explore:

- Dilemmas associated with people's actions and behaviour
- Keeping children safe
- Working with colleagues and other adults

This chapter will investigate dilemmas in areas where problems are common and occur in all sorts of schools, from kindergartens to sixth form colleges.

Our prime concern when working with children and young adults is their safety. When an event occurs where their safety is at risk it can be the most challenging of all problems to deal with. Child safety can be challenged by other children, adults, environments, processes, activities, events and conspiring circumstances. As party leader it is your responsibility to ensure that the safety of your party is constantly appraised and maintained.

The behaviour of children can have a significant effect on the outcome of your trip and the safety of those involved. Difficult children need to be handled carefully, appropriately and within the guidelines set out by your own school. When it comes to other people who might be working with us, such as travel company reps, instructors, parents and the public, we have to work within a less structured framework, and this lack of structural support can be very challenging.

While your colleagues will be mostly supportive and hard working, some can be an absolute nightmare when you have to work with them for a full day, or even a full week. In a few, thankfully extremely rare circumstances, colleagues can be a disruptive and unhelpful influence with their own agendas, or just lazy or incompetent. These people do exist and we have to work with them and around them; knowing how to get the best out of them as a party leader is your challenge.

Keeping children safe

This section presents three areas where party leaders have been challenged while on school trips. They don't represent the full range of child protection issues, rather they present a snapshot of some real situations that have arisen and been dealt with by dedicated teachers.

Case study

Ryan's story

Two of our pupils were in a relationship and wanted to share a room.

Story told by Ryan, a secondary school linguist, about to take 35 male and female year 12 pupils on a tour of the Rhineland with three colleagues.

'I had two female pupils who were in a relationship and they wanted to share a room on our trip along the Rhine in Germany. Their parents knew and were supportive of their relationship and their sharing a room, but

we didn't know quite how to handle things at first. What we didn't want to do was to create a situation where the girls would feel the need to be dishonest and put pressure on their friends to swap rooms without our knowledge, but we felt we also had to be fair to all pupils and those who might be in other kinds of relationship.'

Reflecting on practice

You might think it strange that the parents in this case were so liberal in their attitudes to their daughters' relationship. In fact it is not uncommon for parents to allow their children to engage in sexual relationships with boyfriends and girlfriends at home, and some also expect this to be able to continue on school trips. Despite evidence about sexually transmitted infections (STIs) and a high rate of teenage pregnancy in the UK, attitudes to sex seem to be getting more relaxed. In this case the parents have unwittingly put the staff under pressure to take a decision that perhaps they felt incapable of.

What is the situation in your school?

What is your school policy regarding relationships between pupils?

Do parents unintentionally make it difficult for you to maintain a moral stance?

At first glance it appears to be a pretty straightforward situation: you just say no. There is absolutely no way that you would allow pupils in a heterosexual relationship, whether of legal age or not, to share a room, so why even consider it if they are in a same sex female relationship? Preventing them from 'room hopping' should be fairly straightforward, but on a residential trip the staff can't stay awake for 24 hours just to keep pupils from getting up to mischief can they?

'The girls' parents made the case that they would rather their girls be together sharing a room than make other girls they might share with feel awkward or inconvenienced by having to share a room with them. We made it clear that it was school policy to prevent pupils of any age engaging in sexual activity at any time when involved in school activities. What they did at home, we couldn't control.

We knew the girls well and they would most definitely be a positive addition to the trip in general, but we were stuck on this issue. Let the girls stay together with the blessing of the parents and make it look as though we'd turned a blind eye, or stick to our guns and enforce the school policies? The other option was to encourage them to pull out of the trip.'

When the trip is beneficial to their A-level German studies, making them pull out seems a little harsh. The sticking point here is actually their honesty. Had Ryan and his team been unaware of their relationship, he might have roomed them together anyway, but could easily have grouped them with other girls who might have felt awkward about sharing. If it were two boys in a same sex relationship, would he have had the same dilemma?

'Before we approached the head, we wanted to work out the pros and cons so we could make a suggestion as to the right way forward. What we didn't want to do was to create a problem later on down the line by making the wrong decision. We thought about it from the perspective of a heterosexual couple and then from a homosexual couple. We don't allow pupils in either type of relationship to share because the risk of intentionally or uninten- tionally unprotected penetrative sex is too high. It would be irresponsible for us to allow it.

However, the nature of the relationship that these girls were in, although sexual according to their parents, made the risks of STIs extremely low, or unwanted pregnancy nil.

I should explain that it was the parents' wishes that the girls didn't know we were discussing this issue at such length although they'd requested to share a room on the forms they'd returned.'

Ryan and his team are trying to be too nice here. They recognise that the girls are in a loving and pretty stable relationship by late-teenage standards and want to do the best for them. However, they are being persuaded by a good argument and they need to do what is right rather than what might be popular.

When boys and girls have school trip 'holiday romances' it is pretty easy to spot and to control – remember it's one of our duties as teachers to protect children from making potentially harmful decisions; they may be physically harmful or emotionally harmful. A boy creeping into a girl's room (or vice versa) is a classic school trip problem that many of us have dealt with in the past and it's relatively straightforward to solve. But same sex relationships can be harder to spot and more sensitive to deal with. Ryan and his team clearly don't want to appear 'un-PC' about the nature of the girls' relationship, but they are making a mistake in entertaining the suggestion that they make a special rule for them.

'Because we knew about the relationship we felt we couldn't turn a blind eye. If we had it would have sent a bad message to other pupils who were also in relationships, no matter what type. We didn't end up discussing this issue with the head although we spoke to our child protection officer and he agreed our course of action was clear. In fact we had no choice – we couldn't offer preferential treatment to the girls because we'd be discriminating against those in heterosexual or homosexual relationships if we refused them the same privileges.'

In fact, it was legislation that solved the dilemma for Ryan and his team. It would have been potentially unlawful to discriminate in favour of the girls no matter how good their intentions or the argument from them and their parents. Of course, Ryan and his team were then left with the potential for problems on their trip, but perhaps they and the parents underestimated the girls here.

'We had to explain the situation to the girls and make sure that they could behave sensibly and maintain their relationship in a way that wouldn't impact any potential roommates. It was a pretty easy conversation, all things considered. We got them together with their parents and just explained that we couldn't allow the suggestion on discrimination grounds.'

A happy ending! But I'm sure, as you've been reading this story, you've thought, 'Yes, but what if you discover that a sexual relationship is occurring while you're on a school trip?' Good question, and it's among the most difficult of issues to deal with.

Sex and school trips

It's important that you are guided by school policy and by senior members of staff should you discover an active sexual relationship taking place on your trip. However, it is not unheard of for teenage children to engage in sexual acts even while on day trips.

Case study

Maria's story

We always expect a bit of mucking about on the back seat of the bus, but we'd never have expected what was actually going on …

Story told by Maria, a secondary school English teacher, after a year 10 trip to the theatre with 40 boys and girls.

→

> *'There's always a little bit of noise from the back of the coach on these sort of trips, but this time there seemed to be generally good-natured banter as some of the boys and girls discussed a TV show they'd been watching, not even the play we'd seen, which was disappointing. Anyway, most of the bus was pretty quiet and we nodded off as we travelled down the motorway. We had absolutely no idea what was really going on in the backseat until the next day. It emerged that two of the girls had 'performed an act' on one of the boys as his mate filmed it on his mobile phone. It was all done for a dare! It was discovered in a chemistry lesson when the lad replayed the video to the boy next to him. We'd never have thought anyone would ever do something like that – it was just so extreme.'*

One lesson from this story is that we can't rely on our own moral values and behaviour boundaries when considering younger generations. What we think is acceptable behaviour is often different from those we teach – we were brought up in a different world with different rules and different technology. Easy access to sexual material in electronic media and on mobile phones makes it all too easy for young people to be influenced by, and record, outrageous acts that some children treat as 'a laugh'.

Your child protection officer will help with specific school policies, but if you discover something happening on one of your trips you need to act, but act with care:

- Be discreet and treat the pupils concerned carefully.
- You can't offer confidentiality and you must explain that you'll have to report what you've discovered.
- If any images have been taken you should confiscate the device and seal it in an envelope in front of the owner – don't view the material. You are entitled to confiscate possessions if you feel they are likely to negatively influence a pupil or put them at risk.
- Report the whole thing quickly to your child protection officer and your head and take advice.
- If the children are under the legal age of consent, the parents of one or other may wish to prosecute.
- Act to ensure your pupils' safety and emotional wellbeing.

Having said all of that, perhaps we should make policies on sexual relationships much clearer as we do for drugs and alcohol. No sex on school trips!

Sex education

It's likely that not all teachers are aware of what children in their school know about sex, safe sex and STIs (sexually transmitted infections). Unless you're involved in your school's PSHE programme you may have missed out. But if you're taking a trip where boys and girls could find an opportunity to engage in sexual acts, then it's best that you're aware of what your school does as far as sex education goes.

These websites give a broad understanding of what sort of educational resources exist in the UK and USA:

www.qcda.gov.uk/7203.aspx – guidance from the QCA (qualifications and curriculum authority) in England on sex education in schools.

www.bbc.co.uk/barefacts/sex_education – a UK BBC website for parents.

www.sexetc.org – a US website produced for teenagers by teenagers.

Protecting children from their own bad decisions and pressure from each other is one thing. However, protecting them from other adults is something that the profession has had to become more used to over time. When you are away from home you and your team are the number one defence against negative influences on your pupils – it's not an insignificant responsibility.

Case study

Tanitha's story

We discovered a private guest in our hotel was harassing our pupils.

Story told by Tanitha, a secondary school geography teacher, who took a mixed group of 43 13–18 year olds skiing in Switzerland with four colleagues.

'I've got to say that we didn't feel the trip was going well to start with. We had a number of problems and they just seemed to keep coming one after another. We'd had trouble with the coach on the journey down and had just found out that one of our sixth form lads was a self-harmer and on medication for depression – nobody had told us! It was while I was on the phone home to sort that issue out that I got a bizarre report from three year 10 lads after the afternoon ski session.

We were staying in a pretty grotty hotel; not the one we'd been promised by our tour company, but anyway. Our group was split over two floors →

and on one floor a number of private guests were in rooms close to the kids. Most of them were pleasant enough and kept themselves to themselves. We hadn't had any complaints about the kids from them so we were pretty happy. However, one of the guests was a seasonal worker in the ski resort, who appeared to work at nights in one of the bars; he was always around during the day. The lads claimed he'd been hassling them and inviting them into his room: his door was always open apparently and he could be seen drinking in his room and playing 'shoot-em-up' style video games.

The lads explained that they were just being friendly when they first arrived and went in to play one of the games after dinner the first night while the staff set up a quiz night in the games room. Apparently they'd been a bit 'spooked' by the guy as he had some pornographic material lying around in his room, so they didn't want to go back, but he kept on at them each time they went to their rooms – why they didn't tell us straight away is beyond me.'

Reflecting on practice

What would you do next?

How would you react to such a scenario?

When there is an allegation of an adult attempting to exercise their will over, or exploit, a young person for their own purposes, we tend immediately to jump to the conclusion that the adult must be guilty.

This is a dangerous assumption, as many wrongly accused teachers will testify, but our natural reaction as responsible and caring adults is to want to protect our pupils.

What is your school policy on reporting such allegations?

How could you put that into practice when far from home, maybe overseas?

When I was told this story for the first time, I reacted as you probably are now – it made me feel uncomfortable to think about the boys being at risk from a bad influence in the hotel, where they should feel safe (don't forget that at this stage we don't know the whole story, so we can't judge with confidence). I also felt for Tanitha and imagined the size of the challenge that lay before her.

'I couldn't believe that things were going from bad to worse. I felt like I was really being tested. Far from being a week of fun and relaxation in the mountains, this was turning into an endurance test for me and my staff. I feel a bit selfish saying that, but that's how I felt at the time – apart from being angry at the thought of the kids being at risk like that.

I had to stop myself from reacting straight away and marching up to the room to deal with things there and then. Instead, I asked the boys to write down what they'd told me. I trusted that they weren't making it all up, so I had to act, but I had to do things right or I knew I could make things worse. I didn't feel up to challenging the guy on my own either.

I asked Simon, Olivia and Martin, my colleagues, to join me for a chat over a hot chocolate as the kids arrived back from their lessons and got showered and changed for dinner. I shared what the boys had told me and we discussed the next step. Martin was keen to go straight up to the guy's room and confront him. We didn't feel that was the best option though.'

Indeed no, it wouldn't have been the best option. There are several channels that they could have used to seek help and advice, not least of which is the ski tour company rep and the hotel manager. Perhaps following their emergency protocol would help. A protocol doesn't have to be used exactly as intended; it can be adapted to suit the situation, so they could use their emergency protocol for injuries and adapt it: the same people are likely to be involved – the school emergency contact, the head teacher and possibly the local authorities. The important thing is to follow a plan and work methodically – getting the boys to write down what had happened was a good start. What else?

- Follow a protocol.
- Try to get some background to any allegation before you involve others. Has there been a misunderstanding? Or have others had similar problems?
- Be discreet and act professionally – the *allegations* could be false.
- Never promise confidentiality but do promise discretion, care and tact.
- Agree on specific tactics for dealing with the situation with colleagues – you can't leave them in the dark: you need their help.
- Record all the details religiously. Include everything – times, places, people, even the weather if it helps.
- Consult senior staff about your plan – get agreement and advice.
- Use local knowledge and facilities – travel reps, hotel managers, instructors, etc.
- Involve the police/authorities if you feel it is the right way to solve your problem and provide a safe environment for your pupils.

Tanitha's story continues:

'We all agreed that we needed to take this further. Our tour rep was useless – he'd only just left school himself and we didn't feel that he was worth involving. The hotel manager was never there and the assistant seemed uninterested in our problem. Without help from the hotel staff we felt pretty isolated. We decided that we needed to see for ourselves what the boys had described and try to have a friendly chat with the guy. Simon and Olivia went up to speak to him, leaving Martin to marshal the kids to dinner and me to phone home. We couldn't get anyone to answer at the emergency number and so we tried the head, who was at a golf club dinner but would be given a message to call back. The deputy head was away on a Duke of Edinburgh's trip, but we finally got hold of the head of year 11 who reckoned we needed to involve the local police if what the boys said was true.

Olivia and Simon returned to pretty much confirm what the boys had described – the guy wasn't around but his door was open and it was clear to Simon and Olivia that he wasn't quite the full ticket. We had no choice but to get the assistant manager to call the police.'

Calling the police overseas

Different countries have different law enforcement organisations and it can be confusing as to which one you need. In Italy for example, there are local country police, city police and the famous Carabinieri. Which do you call?

Getting help with this is important – building good relationships from the start with hotel managers, reps and guides and instructors is a good idea – they'll know who can help. Alternatively, do your homework before you go, or talk to someone who's been before.

Tanitha and colleagues took the right approach. Note that she removed Martin from the scene and gave him a job with real purpose, rather than allowing his zeal for protecting the kids to run away with him and further inflame the situation. A good decision!

Involving the authorities need not be a big deal but you need to have your facts straight and be able to explain your grievance as succinctly as possible – your notes will help. If you're not fluent in the local language this can be tricky, but do your best and get help if you need it. Try to avoid using the pupils to translate on sensitive topics, even if they are fluent. Happily, English is a language that is widely learnt in Europe, and Tanitha was lucky enough to be met by a policewoman who spoke perfect English.

'It took them a while to arrive but as soon as they did the police just took over. Three officers arrived and while one listened to our story and wrote down my statement, the other two got the hotel manager in and went up to the guy's room. They left after about 20 minutes and headed off to the bar where he worked and that was the last we heard of him. As far as we could tell he didn't come back, but his room was cleared out and the door shut and locked. We got a grovelling apology from the hotel and the tour company and enjoyed a pretty safe and straightforward trip after that. We just couldn't get over how quickly the situation was dealt with by the police – they were great, they just came in and sorted the problem for us with no fuss at all. We were pretty impressed.'

When booking a trip overseas for a school group, you can do all the right things – go on inspection visits, check out references, visit hotel websites and so on – but you only really know about a place when you get there with your group. In this case the party leader and her group were let down by the tour company and the hotel; they have a responsibility to ensure that their guests do not have a negative impact on each other, and this is particularly important around schoolchildren.

This sort of scenario is unlikely to unfold on one of your trips, but reflecting on how we would deal with something similar provides a challenging test of our readiness to protect our pupils. Unless we consider such scenarios, I would argue that we aren't quite ready to be in charge of a group of children on a trip away from home. You need to have the confidence to know the right thing to do for a given situation. You're unlikely to develop experience of all possible scenarios that could test you, so the next best thing is to reflect on the stories of others, and develop some experience vicariously through them.

Reflecting on practice

Tanitha will have written a report to her head and then the head will have written to the parents of the boys concerned. Is there anything else they should have done following this trip?

Do you think there was anything they could have done to prevent this incident?

Working with colleagues and other adults

For teachers, working with adults can be a refreshing change, as they spend most of their time in the classroom with children and adolescents. The opportunity to engage with colleagues during a shared venture is one that many teachers look forward to. Of course, it's not always plain sailing and I'm sure we can all recall situations where colleagues actually made things more difficult. In some respects, working with your pupils is easier as they will be well used to your *modus operandi* and your specific expectations. You very rarely work hand in glove with your colleagues, so you won't have the same relationship.

Working with adults who aren't colleagues and are new to you also presents problems. Whether it's parents who unintentionally undermine your authority, or travel reps who are as much use as chocolate teapots because they've only just got off the flight before yours, working with people who are unfamiliar with you, your school and the demands of being a teacher can be challenging, or just downright frustrating.

Establishing relationships

Good working relationships develop over time, so you can't expect all the adults on a school trip to know how you work. There will always be someone new and inexperienced in search of guidance or support. Sharing information at the planning stages will help, but you should never expect colleagues to know what you are thinking, or expect them to do what you'd do: we're all different. Follow the guidance in Chapter 2 on good communication practice (see p48) and try to ease new colleagues into the experience.

Working with travel reps or instructors is a different matter. You've got only a couple of hours in some cases to ensure that you can understand how they will work with you and your pupils and how far you can trust them. Consider the following tips.

Working with instructors

- Meet instructors face to face before an activity starts – insist on time for this.
- Get to know names. Try to get the measure of them early on.
- Find out how they intend to work with your pupils.
- Don't be afraid to ask about qualifications and experience – CRB (Criminal Records Bureau) checks, etc.
- Explain your pupil behaviour policy and how you want to be informed if behaviour standards are not met.
- Communicate important information about your pupils that can help – recent injuries, allergies and so on.
- Give them your contact details.
- If you can, meet instructors at breaks and at the end of the day for a debrief. Ensure that they, as well as your pupils, are happy.

Working with travel reps
Before:

- Sales reps of any sort are used to using 'creative truths' to get a sale. Make sure you understand what you are getting into before you go and don't accept promises that have no hope of being honoured.
- Insist that a rep comes to your school to finalise details of your trip.
- Put a name to a face.
- Ask for independent endorsements from other schools *like yours*.

During:

- Insist on, and make time for, a good long chat with your resort rep as soon as you arrive at your destination.
- Don't expect that they'll know everything there is to know about your destination unless they've been there a good while.
- Set out how you want your trip to go – suggest a regular meeting, say over breakfast, so you can discuss how things are going
- Use them as much as you need to.
- Make them feel part of your team – they'll work harder for you and enjoy their time with your party more.

Good relationships with the people you'll be working with are so valuable, but things don't always go to plan.

Case study

Sasha's story

One of our colleagues fell seriously ill while we were in Paris with a large group of year 6 pupils. We had to rethink the whole trip.

Story told by Sasha, a primary school teacher who was part of a team taking 45 year 6 pupils to Disneyland Paris and Paris city centre along with four other members of staff and two parent helpers.

'Our weekend trip itinerary included a day at Disneyland Paris, where we stayed in one of the Disney hotels, and a day in Paris itself to take in the sights before heading home on Eurostar on the Sunday evening – the kids had been buzzing about it for weeks! Despite the rain, everyone had a great day in the park and spent the evening playing games and relaxing before our tour of Paris the next day.

→

> *Later that night I was woken by Tom, who was sharing a room with Dan, our party leader. Dan was having some sort of seizure and the emergency operator that Tom had called on his mobile couldn't speak English. I was the only French speaker (other than Dan) on the staff so Tom called me for help.'*

Reflecting on practice

How many times have you gone to a foreign country without even an idea of the basics of the local language?

Cheap flights and mass tourism have made travel to far-flung corners of the earth incredibly easy. Not understanding the local language is no barrier for us because we tend to expect the people we meet in hotels and restaurants to speak English. But what if they don't?

Shouldn't we make the effort?

Sasha's story is beginning to highlight the problem of isolating expertise in individuals. This phenomenon is almost the polar opposite of the concept of distributed leadership, discussed earlier in Part 1. By isolating knowledge and skill in one person, or having a number of people with different specialisms, the ability of a staff team to react and respond to problems is diminished. While you'd never complain at having a really well-qualified first aider on your trip, or even a doctor, it's not unreasonable to expect the rest of your team to have some skill and knowledge in dealing with injuries: cuts and bruises and other basic procedures. Distribute the leadership *and* distribute the skill.

> *'I'd only been out of teacher training college a year or two and hadn't much experience of dealing with problems like this so I was a little nervous to say the least. Ironically, I was booked on a first aid course the week after the trip, but I didn't really have a clue yet – Dan was our lead first aider but he was on the floor in a bad way. Tom had put him in the recovery position on the floor and covered him in a blanket.'*

Again, the skills seem to have been isolated in one individual. Dan, the guy in trouble on the floor, is the lead first aider and must surely be out of action for the rest of the trip if he's in a bad way – so who provides first aid cover for the rest of the 45 kids and four staff?

> *'The ambulance arrived pretty quickly, and the paramedics were sure that Dan had had an epileptic attack. We hadn't known about his condition before so we were all pretty shaken up. We kept things pretty quiet as he was treated as we didn't want to worry the kids.*

Tom and Patricia, who were my senior colleagues, took charge and sent me off to hospital with Dan so that I could communicate with the medics – Dan had been out for the count for a while and was pretty dazed, although he was starting to come round. I grabbed his bag, passport and health insurance card and jumped in the ambulance.'

Good. Dan has been well looked after and there has been a seamless leadership succession from him to Tom and Patricia, who will stay in the hotel with the kids and the remaining member of staff and two parents. Five adults for 45 children still gave a good level of supervision (1:9) and allowed them to carry on with the trip the next day.

'I arrived back at the hotel having spoken to Dan and the doctors. He was OK and chatting but was tired and was being kept in for observation as it was his first epileptic episode – that's why we didn't know. I just had time to shower and change before we took the kids to breakfast and started the journey into the centre of Paris.

Patricia had phoned Dan's wife and we'd stayed in contact with each other while Dan was being treated at the accident and emergency department. Dan's wife was flying out later in the day to meet him; she was a bit shaken up but otherwise keen to be there.

As the only French speaker on the trip, Tom and Patricia gave me the respon-sibility of leading the group around Paris!'

The trip leader has been incapacitated and can't carry on with his responsibilities, so he's been left behind to be met by his wife. The youngest and most inexpe-rienced teacher has just arrived back at 6am, has had no sleep and, as the only language specialist on the staff, has just been given the responsibility of leading the rest of the trip. Poor girl! The workload seems to have been spread a little thick in one area, doesn't it? Why? Have Tom and Patricia got the wrong idea about leadership and just decided to delegate and stand back and take the credit for making the decisions?

'The coach driver did a great job of taking us from place to place. We managed stops in the Champs Elysées, at the Arc de Triomphe, Notre Dame and even went up the Eiffel Tower. I led each stop and liaised over paying for tickets and took a group of nine kids around each spot. When we arrived at the station to take the train home I was pretty pleased with my work – I'd been awake for 35 hours, had only been teaching two years and had managed to keep the trip going. I didn't mind that Tom and Patricia were going to get the credit for taking over when we got home, I was just pleased to see the station.

We arrived at the ticket barriers and Tom turned to me and asked me where the tickets were. I had no idea – I thought he had them. It turned out that the tickets were in Dan's bag, with Dan, in hospital. "You were supposed to bring them back with you," said Patricia. Nobody told me!'

It just gets worse and worse! Sasha has worked her heart out to help deal with a tricky situation and seems to have done a pretty good job. We've only got her word for it, but we've no reason to suggest that her version isn't accurate.

The problem here appears to be centred on the succession of leadership and a lack of communication during a difficult and stressful period. There was no contingency for this sort of situation so protocol wasn't on people's minds when it all went wrong. It's fair enough that everyone was focused on Dan's health, but the situation needed a cool head to work out an essential plan for the next step. Instead it looks as though everyone but Sasha went to bed and hoped for the best. Oh dear!

This story doesn't necessarily suggest that the trip was badly organised, or that the staff who took over did a bad job, or even that Sasha was particularly heroic. Indeed, we can be sure that the staff and two parents did everything they could to ensure that the rest of the trip went well and that the kids got home with smiles on their faces. Incidentally, they did manage to get on the train, but only by sweet talking the ticket office to call head office and explain the situation.

What the story does suggest is that, regardless of what Dan had planned and how good his logistical organisation was, the staff continued to work together as though they were in school, where you can 'wing it' to a certain extent because you can always hastily organise support if you need it. However, being away from school means that you need to work with colleagues in a different manner.

- Rather than trying to lead by delegating most of the work to a junior colleague in the same way you might delegate photocopying, Tom and Patricia could have shared the leadership roles by focusing on everyone's skills rather than those of just one person.

- The team expected Dan to lead them. Maybe they imagined that they were there for pupil herding and 'helping', but by thinking this they've excused themselves of any responsibility. If Dan hadn't given them sufficient detail about their roles on the trip they should have asked. Instead they bumbled through expecting one person to lead from the front.

- While we all have particular strengths in school, be they subject specific, sporting, pastoral or academic, there are some schoolteacher skills that we all possess – marshalling pupils around, dealing with behaviour, etc. Those skills still count, but on a school trip you need more – it's no good one person having all the skills you need. You want a liberal sprinkling of the skills and knowledge needed to complete the trip. You need to meet up and decide what's required.

- Subject or key stage leaders in schools will be expert in their fields and possess knowledge and access to information that classroom teachers may not. These middle leaders are proficient at filtering information (exam board paperwork, etc.) so that classroom teachers can function as they need to. It's right that they should do that – a need-to-know system has its place – but not when you are far from home. Sharing information and authority is essential.

- Essential stuff like tickets, passports, medical details, parental contact information and transport and destination contact details are all recommended in Chapter 2 as things that all your team should have access to and know what to do with. In Sasha and Dan's story they were all in his bag, just as all the SATs data or exam board paperwork might be in the head of department's filing cabinet. The 'team' relied too heavily on one person, first Dan and then Sasha.

Reflecting on practice

Is there anything in the analysis above that you connect with?

Are you challenged to think about your own experience in a new way?

Might this story offer an opportunity to extend your future practice?

Did Tom and Patricia miss the point of leadership by getting Sasha to do all the work, or do you think they made the most of her strengths as a linguist?

Case study

Callum's story

The head wants us to take a member of the SMT with us on our trip in case anything goes wrong. He thinks that the current team is too young and inexperienced to deal with problems on its own.

Story told by Callum, a sixth form college lecturer taking an art trip to Barcelona with 25 male and female students and three other members of staff (two female and one male).

'We're teachers in the art and modern languages departments. Both departments are quite young and the school has a pretty big turnover of staff each year, so there are lots of NQTs in the staffroom. The people teaching the art course and the Spanish language specialist are all under 25, and while I've been teaching for eight years already (I'm 30), we're apparently too young to take the trip on our own. The head called me in to her office following receipt of my trip proposal form to tell me that she thought we needed more experienced staff on the trip. I haven't told the other guys yet cos they'll probably refuse to go. It's a real insult.'

On the one hand, if the head says 'jump', you jump. On the other hand, there really should be a good reason for you to involve SMT staff who have no expertise in relation to your trip. Say you are taking a ski or scuba diving trip, how much help would a senior member of staff be if they have no experience or interest in skiing or scuba diving? If they wanted to learn with the rest of the group, then that would be fine, but they'd have to defer authority to their instructors – could they do that? On an art trip to Barcelona there is much that a non-specialist senior manager would find interesting in the many Gaudi attractions and the Picasso Museum – they might even learn from their junior colleagues, but that doesn't appear to be the motivation behind this request from the head. It's clear that there is an implied element of checking up on the junior staff in this case. Moving forward with some questions might help:

1. Are there any specific reasons for the decision other than a supposed lack of experience?
2. Is there anything that the head or members of your staff team aren't telling you?
3. Who has the head got in mind? Could they actually be helpful?

If there is a good reason for the head to ask you to take a member of the SMT, then you can work with it. Has there ever been any misconduct on any previous trips? Any high levels of injury? Any serious behaviour problems? Are any of the staff on probation for any reason? If the answer is no to all of these questions then it would seem unclear as to why the head isn't happy with your arrangements. Even if your team is entirely made of post-probationary year NQTs and you're the only 'experienced' member of staff, you've still got a team of fully trained and qualified teachers to work with, so what's the problem?

Callum's story continues:

> 'Our head is relatively new having only started last year and the chair of governors is keen that the school stays out of the papers unless it's good news. In a meeting that she reluctantly agreed to, the head told me that she was worried about alcohol abuse among the kids and wanted a figure of authority on the trip who could dissuade them from poor behaviour. Apparently a language exchange last year had been a bit of a disaster after two of the teachers had been out drinking with the kids and some of the host families.
>
> I felt a little annoyed that I wasn't considered authoritative enough and that we were being treated as though we were already guilty of something. So there was no good reason other than a suspicion that we might have similar trouble because our team was so young.'

It's important for all staff, even a head, to defer to your leadership in your area of expertise. If that includes your trip then you're the boss – people should trust you. However, all trips from schools operate under the authority of the head and so their opinion counts. Nevertheless, it's important that you and your staff are recognised as competent, even expert, in your field. Having, to all intents and purposes, an uninvited member of the SMT on your trip sends a poor message to your staff and to you, suggesting that your school leaders don't have any faith or trust in your abilities.

'What the head didn't appreciate was that we would have to ask one of the existing team to step down from the trip in order for the SMT member to come along as the staff places were allocated on a 1:10 ratio. With four staff we were already two staff over that so we'd had to pay for the extra staff by raising the price per pupil. This gave us a great staff/pupil ratio and enabled better tuition when we got to the museums and other sites of interest. Of course, if the school would pay extra for another room in the hotel, travel and museum entry costs then at least that would be one less headache.

The school wouldn't pay! I had no choice, either cancel the trip or allow Mr or Mrs SMT to join us and drop one of my colleagues who'd helped in the planning stages.'

Making compromises and taking difficult decisions is part and parcel of organising a trip – we have to jump through all sorts of hoops and satisfy a range of different people in positions of authority to get a trip off the ground – but rarely do heads interfere in this way. Poor old Callum is faced with a difficult dilemma here. Don't forget that he's under no obligation to take a trip at all; he could just say enough is enough and walk away. But we don't organise these sorts of learning ventures because we have to – we want to because they are valuable and helpful to our pupils.

What the head is asking here seems unfair, but she's reacting to concerns raised in previous similar trips and wants to ensure that this one goes well. Maybe she's a little overcautious in her first few years as a head, but we can forgive that, can't we? Nevertheless, it wouldn't hurt her to make her loyal and professional staff feel valued.

Callum has a choice to make here:

Go ahead with the head's request.

Or:

Leave it a while and resubmit a reworked proposal in a way that will allay any fears or worries that the head might have.

Or:

Cancel the trip.

Cancelling the trip seems like a last resort and it doesn't really provide a solution to the problem. Asking the head for more time to think it over before going ahead might be the better option. While taking the SMT member along might not be a problem at all, no matter who it is, the young team's enthusiasm and confidence are going to be adversely affected. In my opinion, heads need to avoid damaging morale and enthusiasm in young teachers, no matter what their intentions. In my experience beginning teachers react well to responsibility and thrive in situations where they feel trusted and in control. However, they do this best when operating within a supportive and guiding professional culture. Is such a culture in evidence in Callum's school I wonder? Teaching is a business loaded full of expectations of responsibility and now accountability, and while the GTC's (General Teaching Council for England) code of conduct and practice for registered teachers is helpful in this regard it is vital that schools develop a culture that fosters good practice and professional behaviour too.

GTC code of conduct and practice for registered teachers in England

The development of the code of conduct has been accompanied by much controversy as something that is trying to control teachers' lives beyond school. It's much less worrying than that in practice. It sets out what we should be able to expect in a professional teacher and is actually open to a great deal of interpretation, which means that any action taken as a result of an alleged breach of the code needs to take account of the specific unique circumstances. (See http://www.gtce.org.uk/teachers/thecode/.)

Can the head teacher in this case develop such a culture without placing her trust in young teachers? Surely such a culture and the expression of clear and collaboratively derived guidelines for professional behaviour on school trips, carefully communicated to all and embedded in practice, is better than having 'a grown-up' watch over young teachers. We all want people to join the profession who can 'hit the ground running' and inspire pupils with their enthusiasm. A school culture and structure that nurtures this is what's needed. Callum realised this too:

'It became clear that we were going to have to prove ourselves if we were going to take the sort of trip that we wanted – a relaxed and effective artistic and cultural experience where the kids and staff could reflect on, and produce, art together in an inspirational environment.

We sat down together and discussed why the head thought we needed a more experienced teacher to come along. I told the team about the drinking on the language exchange and as I expected they felt a bit aggrieved that they were "painted with the same brush". However, as we talked, it became clear that school trips were never explicitly mentioned during their NQT induction and probationary year. Each of the team had different experiences during their PGCEs so they hadn't received consistent guidance on professional behaviour in school, let alone on school trips.'

We expect teachers to know how to behave; they are pillars of the community and some people look up to them as role models. But it's reasonable to expect guidance on what is professional behaviour to be clearly articulated. In the case of Callum and his young team, it was never clearly articulated in their school and seems to be at the crux of the issue.

'We thought we had something here so we trawled through the school policies and nothing came up that explained what it was to be professional on school trips. There was a brief mention of what it was to be negligent in the staff disciplinary issues policy but that was it.

We met again and roughed out a policy for what parents could expect of teachers when taking their children away on school trips. We wrote it a bit like a manifesto if you like; a set of promises that we would do our very best to keep. It included a kind of what if FAQ section which we thought might be as helpful to us as it would to parents. We were careful not to promise too much as accidents can happen despite the best laid plans and things do go wrong.

Along with our rewritten proposal, we presented our policy to the head ...'

Brilliant! No matter whether the head liked it or not, the act of sitting down together to really think hard about practice must have been so useful to them all.

TOP TIP!

Finding time to get together to sit and think about professional practice is tricky, especially now that many colleagues have lots of different responsibilities in one school and the working week directive restricts hours. Why not try to turn your meeting into a social event? Discuss the issues over a meal – dinner, lunch or even breakfast. Coffee breaks are never long enough but are good times to get hold of people.

If you want to make changes and improve practice you'll need to make sacrifices somewhere along the line – your free time during the day is the first place to start. It is worth it though.

Through their attempts to contribute to their school's professional practice framework they are strengthening the professional culture at the same time, but not restricting enthusiasm and damaging morale. They've generated knowledge about their profession and provided guidance for others. However, these initiatives only work if they are adopted by those in authority. If they are, perhaps with a few tweaks here and there, then the school can be said to be developing a collaborative culture within which leadership is distributable.

> 'It took a while for the head to get back to us, but after two weeks she called us all into her office to quiz us one at a time on our proposed school trip manifesto. The meeting went well – she appeared to be interested in how much we all knew about it and whether we knew what to do if something went wrong. We'd submitted a detailed risk assessment, but she seemed to want to test us on it. Fair enough I suppose, but we sailed through the meeting, no problem!'

It's unusual for a head to call teachers into their office to discuss a trip. Normally an EVC (educational visits coordinator) might run through some of the details with you, but that would be about it. However, in this case Callum and his team are trying to contribute to whole school practice and by doing so give trust and responsibility to the many younger staff in the school. It's a new development and needs to be carefully thought about, maybe even at governing body level before it is adopted.

> 'With a few changes and a number of additions to our manifesto we were given permission to run our trip as we'd planned. I think that the head could see our point of view and, although she'd never quite admitted to lacking trust in our ability she now felt more comfortable with what we were going to do. To be honest, she doesn't get much time to get to know how we work, so she was only being cautious in the first place.'

This is the best outcome that could have been hoped for, even better than if Callum's head hadn't intervened in the first place. The result is a trip that can go ahead as the originators had planned, a team with renewed confidence and a sense of self-efficacy and a worthwhile contribution to school policy and the professional culture.

It would have been all too easy to let the situation get to the team, for them just to walk away and adopt a defiant position. But they persevered and looked positively at the situation. It was wise of Callum to look at an alternative solution and be creative in his approach, while involving the younger staff in the development of the manifesto was extremely beneficial, particularly for their own professional development. I would now suggest that developing such a manifesto is good practice, that parents and senior managers in schools should know what to expect from teachers on school trips specifically, and that this should be communicated across a school staffroom. You wouldn't write such a document to be accountable as such but to help answer questions that parents and others might have, such as:

1. How will my son/daughter be cared for?
2. How will my son's/daughter's safety be assured?
3. What professional behaviour can I expect from the supervising staff?
4. How will the supervising staff assess risk?
5. What are the risks?
6. What level of supervision can I expect?
7. What will happen if something goes wrong?
8. How will I be contacted if I'm needed?
9. How will the supervising staff deal with an emergency?
10. What should I agree to when sending my son/daughter on a school trip?
11. What are my rights and responsibilities?

As well as dealing superbly with the head teacher, Callum and his team have developed a way of providing more information to parents and creating a better channel for them to communicate with teachers. Teachers in his school can benefit from the protocols that emerge from the new manifesto and can fine-tune their work to continue to improve how they organise school trips.

TOP TIP!

If something doesn't work at your school, why not fix it? Work with others and make things better. Don't be afraid of the nay-sayers, get on and improve – you'll just leave them behind.

Reflecting on practice

Connect–challenge–extend?

You may not have come across a similar situation yourself, but consider how your school trips help NQTs to develop their skills. Or if you're an NQT yourself, consider how you could benefit from the type of work that Callum and his team were involved in. If you've got an idea for a trip, get some advice and make a plan.

Could you influence how you and your colleagues work for the better?

Do you talk about what you do with your colleagues?

Do you move forward with new ideas or stick with the tried and tested?

Conclusion

Dealing with children, even the well-behaved ones, has its challenges. However, working with other adults can be the most stressful and challenging aspect of your job. Nevertheless, if you've got an idea for something new, you'll have to work with men and women in your school to get things done. If you're out and about, you'll have to work with people you may have met only that day, so forging relationships and teams is difficult in and out of school.

People around you can pose a threat to your trip, but they can also enhance it. However, when you're out on a school trip, you are the responsible adult who is ensuring that the children or young adults in your care are protected from harm, so you have to make judgements about where is safe and who is safe to be around.

The stories told in this chapter reflect others' experiences that have led to a change in the way they run their trips. The lessons learnt here can be applied to your next venture out of school and could help to make it more of a success than you'd imagined. Good and bad things can happen to people on your trip and around it. If you can minimise the potential for bad things to happen then you'll do an excellent job, have a great trip and come back full of enthusiasm for the next one.

The stories in Chapter 6 represent occasions where colleagues have learnt to deal with situations that might be specific to the places they find themselves in. It will deal with stories about travelling from place to place and the challenges that can crop up along the way, as well as the great outdoors and the particular hazards that accompany its great beauty.

Key ideas summary

- You have a duty to protect children and young adults from sources of harm, whether from persons unknown, themselves or hazardous situations.

- Treating parents and senior management as though they are clients can focus your planning.

- Have the confidence to ask for help when you need it – know where to get it when you're on your trip.

- Get to know people. Working with people in an effective manner requires good communication, compromise, respect, creativity and patience.

- NQTs need opportunities to lead trips and gain experience outside the school.

- School trips are a great source of CPD.
- Thinking through the challenges of your trip with your colleagues can contribute to your school's professional development culture.

Going further

Further reading on child protection

Calder, M.C. (2008) *Contemporary Risk Assessments in Safeguarding Children* (London: Russell House).

DfES (2006) *Working Together to Safeguard Children: A guide to inter-agency working to safeguard and promote the welfare of children* (London: HMSO).

Fitzgerald, D. and Kay, J. (2007) *Working together in Children's Services* (London: David Fulton).

Munro, E. (2008) *Effective Child Protection* (London: Sage).

Research and reading on working with colleagues

Hargreaves, A. (1992) Cultures of Teaching: A focus for change. In Hargreaves, A. and Fullan, M. (eds), *Understanding Teacher Development* (London: Cassell).

Hindin, A., Morocco, C., Mott, E. and Aguilar, C. (2007) More Than Just a Group: Teacher collaboration and learning in the workplace, *Teachers and Teaching: Theory and Practice*, 13 (4), 349–376.

Joyce, B. and Showers, B. (1988) *Student Achievement Through Staff Development* (White Plains, NY: Longman).

Kolb, D. (1984) *Experiential Learning: Experience as the source of learning and development* (Englewood Cliffs, NJ: Prentice-Hall).

McLaughlin, C., Black-Hawkins, K., McIntyre, D. and Townsend, A. (2008) *Networking Practitioner Research* (Abingdon: Routledge).

Moon, J. (2004) *A Handbook of Reflective and Experiential Learning* (London: RoutledgeFalmer).

Pedder, D., Storey, A. and Opfer, V. (2008) *Schools and Continuing Professional Development (CPD) in England – State of the Nation research project* (London: TDA).

Pickering, J., Daly, C. and Palcher, N. (2007) (eds) *New Designs for Teachers' Professional Learning* (London: Institute of Education).

Rosenholtz, S. (1989) *Teachers' Workplace: The social organization of schools* (New York: Teachers' College Press).

Timperley, H., Wilson, A., Barrar, H. and Fung, I. (2007) *Teacher Professional Learning and Development: Best evidence synthesis iteration* (Wellington, New Zealand: Ministry of Education).

Wilson, E. and Demetriou, H. (2007) New Teacher Learning: Substantive knowledge and contextual factors, *Curriculum Journal*, 18 (3), 213–229.

The challenge of travelling with children and the 'great outdoors'

What this chapter will explore:

- Travel problems
- The great outdoors

In this chapter you will gain a better understanding of how to lead your group through challenges that are presented when travelling and being in the great outdoors. It will enable you to learn from others' triumphs and mistakes and reflect on your own experience.

The location of your trip can present some interesting and unique challenges. If you are travelling over any kind of distance, you'll most likely encounter some of the types of places discussed in this chapter.

However, if you mostly take domestic day trips, don't think that lessons learnt from longer trips, sports tours or expeditions can't apply to you. Much of what we can learn is directly transferable, along with the tactics and strategies for dealing with problems.

While interesting, the actual situations described aren't that important – it's the nature of the challenge that is important, whether it's dealing with an environment, people or a situation beyond your control.

Travel problems

For any school trip the first and last hurdles to overcome involve travel of some form. You may be walking, flying or even sailing; whatever you do, doing it with a group of children of any age can be a challenge, especially if there are 40 or so of them!

Chapter 3 explored a range of travel options and considered their pros and cons at some length. The most common form of travel is probably the minibus or coach, but increasingly schools are using low cost airlines to widen pupils' horizons and expand the possibilities for educational experiences.

Flying means travelling to the airport, checking in with the right weight of baggage, going through security and passport control, boarding the plane, and roughly repeating the process the other side, then doing it all again on the way home. The more complex the process, the greater the chance of something going wrong.

The two stories that follow represent challenges that arise from events that are completely out of the control of the party leaders. It was up to them to react and do their best to achieve a satisfactory outcome from a situation that they could not have foreseen.

Case study

Kenneth's story

Our flight was diverted – 150 miles away from our intended destination and where the parents were expecting to meet their children.

Story told by Kenneth, a middle-school teacher returning to the UK after an orchestra concert tour to Rome with 45 year 6 and 7 pupils, five colleagues and lots of luggage.

→

> 'We'd all settled down on the plane after an excellent tour to Rome; we'd played six concerts in four days and had had fantastic weather too. We had just taken off when the pilot came on the PA to tell us we were being diverted because of damage to the runway at our intended airport. The nearest diversion was 150 miles away!'

Many of us have been in similar situations I'm sure. Diversions and delays are a fact of life for travellers, but with 45 children in tow they can be a real challenge, especially when all the staff are tired after a busy trip. Tempers can fray from time to time. Delays aren't so bad, as all you can do is sit tight or at the very worst (or best depending on your point of view) check into a hotel at the airline's expense. The worst kind of delay is when you are on your way home, and your pupils are running out of money and you feel like you're on your last legs. Somehow, you have to make sure everyone is fed and watered and safe. In Kenneth's story they didn't have the luxury of knowing they were being diverted before they got on the plane, so they couldn't pre-warn parents.

> 'It was only when we landed at 9pm that night that we could get in contact with parents to say that our arrival plans had changed. Naturally, we asked the kids to use their mobile phones, but there were some we just couldn't contact. Because we'd made plans for the kids to be met by their parents at the airport we had no onward transport plans. So we were stuck 150 miles from home.'

It's not unreasonable not to have a plan B for this kind of scenario as you wouldn't know where a diversion airport is likely to be – it's just too much of a guess. The best you can plan for is the need to contact all parents quickly.

TOP TIP!

Use the 'pyramid trickle-down' method for contacting big numbers of people quickly:

- Organise your pupils' parents into groups of four or five.
- Give the first person on the list the numbers of five people.
- That parent will call those five.
- Each one of the five will contact a further five.
- And so on.

Before doing this you need to make sure that all parents agree for their phone numbers to be distributed among the parental group.

This is for general information only – bad news of any kind should always come from the head teacher.

In a situation like this you must ensure that communication with parents is crystal clear. It's possible that some parents might have been studying the arrival details, realised the change of destination and started driving 150 miles. That's fine, unless you've organised something different – you don't want to pass them on the other side of the motorway as you make your way home.

> 'The airline offered to transfer us to the original airport in taxis, but we were a party of 45 and we couldn't ensure supervision and safety of our pupils in a fleet of taxi cabs on their own. And in any case we had luggage and musical instruments to get back too.'

In all fairness to the airline, they are offering a fair service, but they have not taken into account the nature of their passengers on this occasion. A group of adults travelling back in taxis is one thing, children is quite another. While a licensed taxi cab driver is unlikely to pose any threat to the safety of your pupils, you just shouldn't take the risk – should you?

> 'Even if the taxi company had been able to provide seven seaters we couldn't have got everyone in along with a member of staff. I tried to explain this to the guy behind the customer service desk but he wouldn't budge on the issue as the taxi firm had a contract with the airline and couldn't offer anything bigger than three seven seaters and the rest in four seaters. I just wasn't happy with it and time was ticking on. Luckily our pyramid trickle-down contact protocol had worked and parents were staying put for now. But we were sat there trying to decide how to offer proper care for the kids and get home as the rest of the passengers on the flight sped away in taxis.'

Kenneth is right to stand his ground and not just accept what's on offer without really thinking about it.

Reflecting on practice

There are three pressing needs that can be identified in this story:

1. That the pupils need to get home to meet their parents.
2. That the pupils travel in a safe manner.
3. That the party leader exercises some control over how needs 1 and 2 are fulfilled.

To ensure that the children get home in safety, a method of transit must be chosen that the party leader can quickly assess as safe and acceptable. His options are as follows:

(a) Accept the offer from the airline to taxi kids.

→

(b) Stay put and ask parents to collect the children with a two and a half hour wait until they arrive.

(c) Organise something himself with the likelihood that he'll have to pay for it there and then and claim on the insurance once it's all over.

What course would you follow – a, b or c?

Kenneth's story continues:

'I have to admit that I was getting a bit fed up with the situation and was annoyed by the lack of help that the airline was giving us. Anyway, after a bit of a brainstorm with my colleagues on the trip we decided to go it alone and see if we could find any taxi firms with minibus sized taxis. We grabbed the last two seven seaters that the original taxi firm had and sent the 12 youngest kids and two members of staff off in the direction of home. The remaining 33 children stayed with us while we rang around the local taxi firms to find minibus-sized taxis – we couldn't find them. We kept coming up with seven seaters!'

So the idea of doing their own thing is looking a little dodgy now that they've lost two supervising members of staff, as 33 children leaves them with a ratio of 1:8.25, and there weren't any 9.25 seater (8.25 children plus 1 staff) taxis around.

'At this point we finally got through to our emergency contact at school, who agreed that we were right not to send the kids off in taxis alone. As we were talking she had a brainwave and remembered that an ex-colleague of ours worked in a school nearby – maybe they had a 16-seater minibus we could use. She hung up, then called back a minute later to say that Sarah was on her way to pick up 15 kids and a member of staff and she could take us most of the way if the parents drove to meet us at an agreed service area on the motorway. That left us with the possibility of getting three more seven seaters plus one smaller cab to get us all back home. We hurriedly booked them and got them on their way as the minibus arrived.

Thank goodness for our connections with Sarah and her head's permission, or we would have been really stuck! The pyramid trickle-down phone system came into its own again and the parents met their kids as planned. We had a little bit of paperwork to do with the insurance company about reimbursing our colleague's school for diesel and paying for the cabs, but it was worth it to get home safely.'

Kenneth's story is one that starts with confusion and disappointment, gets bogged down in number crunching and phone calls and finally rejoices in the benefits of having an extended network of colleagues willing to help out fellow professionals.

One very effective system that this party leader used was the 'pyramid trickle-down' idea. It relies on a team effort and can be tricky to set up, but when instructions change so often in situations like this it is a very powerful, fast and no-nonsense communication tool.

The emergency contact came into her own in this example too. In high pressure situations when people are tired and becoming irritable they can miss the simplest of solutions to problems. It's daft but we don't tend to look to other schools for help – they're the competition. But why shouldn't we? Why not let colleagues from other schools use our school car parks when they are visiting our town, or share minibuses and drivers? It can't hurt can it?

Case study

Ingrid's story

We had to stop in the middle of nowhere with smoke coming out of the engine of our coach.

Story told by Ingrid, a primary school year 4 class teacher on her way back from a class history trip to the Tower of London with 29 children, two other class teachers, a classroom assistant and two parents.

'Our year 4 trip to the Tower of London had gone really well; the kids were buzzing about the dungeons and the suits of armour and Traitors Gate, not to mention the Beefeaters and their funny uniforms. That was until the coach broke down on the motorway on the way home. The driver pulled over to the hard shoulder and we rolled to a stop by a steep bank and a couple of hundred yards from a bridge over the road. The driver got out, wandered around the bus and got on the phone to his depot. He then leaned over his seat and told us we'd have to wait for the recovery truck and a spare coach to come and pick us up. The best we could do was to sit tight until they turned up.'

Is that the best he could do? It doesn't sound very helpful, and in any case how has he taken the safety of his passengers into consideration? Buses are great big metal boxes but they're not unbreakable, so is it the best idea to sit tight at the side of the motorway as heavy goods vehicles thunder past in the inside lane?

Reflecting on practice

What sort of advice would you want to receive from a coach driver if you were in a similar situation?

What about safety, quality of service, communication and information?

What are you going to do about pick-up times from school?

Ingrid's story continues:

> 'We weren't happy with his explanation and didn't know how long it might take to get a replacement bus. We weren't keen on sitting tight because we'd always been told to leave a car and climb the banking to get away from the vehicle in case it was hit. The driver didn't seem to know about that and was being difficult about the timings. It was difficult for him to be precise so we kind of understood, but it still wasn't good enough.'

Ingrid is in a difficult situation where she doesn't feel confident about what to do, but she knows that the current arrangement while the coach is broken down at the side of the road isn't right.

What are her options? Does she:

Phone the school and tell someone to phone the parents to let them know they'll be late, accept that the driver knows best and sit down and wait as he suggests?

Or:

Assess the risks there and then and form a plan that she thinks is better, then phone the school to explain what she's going to do and then get them to phone parents?

Or:

Is there a third option?

> 'To be honest I felt a little unsure of what to do – we knew the replacement coach had a long way to come and we didn't fancy sitting in the coach on the hard shoulder. We couldn't quite decide whether it was safer to stay put or get the kids off and up the banking. After a quick chat with colleagues we decided to get out and get the kids away from the bus and take control of the situation ourselves. When we did, the driver finally became useful and helped us marshal the kids off – we formed a kind of staff tunnel up the bank between the five of us while Jo collected the kids at the top and they climbed over the fence into a farmer's field, settling under a tree with all their warm coats on. It was drizzling but not too cold so we thought they'd be OK.'

Ingrid and her team show good command and control skills here after finally making the decision to take charge and get the kids away. The tunnel idea is great thinking as it offers excellent control in a really dangerous environment and comfort and reassurance to the children. Getting the safe side of the fence was a good idea too because it allows the teachers to feel more relaxed about the control of their group as the fence provides a physical barrier and it's easy to spot a child climbing over it.

> 'Meanwhile Jennifer went to phone the traffic police on one of the orange phones at the side of the road. We thought it best to let them know that we had 29 kids at the side of the road and get some professional help. A big 4x4 arrived about 20 minutes later and the two highways officers were great – they had a few blankets for the kids to snuggle up under and made sure that we were all OK. Knowing that the kids were at a safe distance and seeing the flashing lights made me feel better: the officers said we'd done the right thing, although I was nervous about taking charge in the driver's domain – he did give me a few dirty looks.'

Having established leadership of the situation, Ingrid's confidence has returned and she feels more in control – the children are all in one place and away from a hazard that she assessed on the spot and controlled in an appropriate manner. She followed her gut instinct and supported it with knowledge, experience and good judgement. Getting professional help from highways officers was a master stroke – she could so easily have sat and waited while everyone got cold and miserable.

Here's what Ingrid did well:

- She followed her instincts concerning the safety of her pupils.
- She took decisive action to improve a situation.
- She assessed the risk there and then and addressed it with appropriate control.
- She acted confidently and took charge of the situation and the 29 children that she and her colleagues were charged with protecting.
- Her leadership *improved* a situation.

Ingrid's story ends well: the replacement coach turned up and everyone got home safe, if a little tired. While breaking down is usually a mere inconvenience for most motorists, as Ingrid's short story demonstrates it presents a much bigger challenge when you have lots of other people's children to care for. But it could easily have been worse:

Parents demand answers after children escape Stortford school bus blaze

PARENTS are demanding answers after a Bishop's Stortford school bus caught fire this morning (Monday, March 16).

The driver and 48 schoolchildren from St Mary's Catholic School in Wind Hill escaped uninjured when fire gutted the SM Coaches bus. It caught alight on the A414 near the turn-off for the Hadhams shortly after 8am.

St Mary's assistant headteacher Emmanuel Bonich and parents have praised Year 11 and Sixth Form students for ushering younger pupils off the bus. "They were very commendable in their actions; very calm and caring and took decisive action", he said. Many of the children were too distressed to continue with their journey to school.

Martin Scarry, whose 11-year-old son James was on the bus, and who submitted [his] mobile phone footage [to the website], said he had been complaining about health and safety issues surrounding the school bus for months. Three fire engines – one from Ware, one from Hertford and a crew from Harlow – attended the scene. The blaze was extinguished by 9.14am. One eyewitness said: "It was awful. I was driving past and I saw all the kids up on the bank. The flames were huge. I've never seen anything like that before – only on television. It's amazing that no-one was injured."

Gary Sanderson, spokesman for the East of England Ambulance Service, said: "On our arrival the school coach was ablaze. Approximately 40 children who were on the coach were led to a place of safety and there were no injuries." A paramedic ambulance was placed on standby at the scene while fire-fighters brought the blaze under control.

Herts County Council spokeswoman said: "The vehicle has been removed for investigation by the police and the Vehicle Operator Standards Agency. No further comment on the cause of the incident is available while the investigation is underway. We expect to have results within two weeks."

(Story courtesy of Herts & Essex Observer newspaper: www.hertsandessexobserver.co.uk)

It was wonderful that nobody was injured and that all the children got off the bus safely. But this was a daily bus journey that took place to and from school with no adults other than the driver to supervise. It just goes to show how well children can deal with real crises themselves and act in a mature manner when under great pressure.

Reflecting on practice

Knowing when to take over in a difficult situation is tricky. We assume that someone who does something for a living, like driving a coach or instructing on a climbing wall, knows their stuff. But what if you're not happy with their work? How do you step in and at what point?

It's difficult to judge, particularly if you don't have any expertise in what's going on. Could you rely on your instincts and make a decision?

The simplest way to think about any situation like Ingrid's is to ask the following questions:

1. Is the current situation safe, acceptable and beneficial to the children?
2. Could it be improved?
3. Can I improve it by intervening?

If, after some thought and assessment, you can answer no, yes and yes, then go ahead and make a change. If you don't feel confident enough to throw your metaphorical weight around, then get together with a colleague and work as a team.

Never be afraid to politely ask someone to change what they are doing if you are not happy with the service your pupils are receiving.

The great outdoors

Bad weather

While there are many dangers in the great outdoors, weather tends to be the most common component of problems when out and about.

If you've lived in the British Isles for any length of time, you'll know how changeable the weather can be: hailstones in July, bright sunshine in December, sudden tropical style downpours, snow in May, floods – we get it all here. It is the prudent and intelligent party leader who considers the weather as a vital part of any venture out of doors.

If you are caught in bad weather such as pouring rain and your pupils get wet, they can be at risk of suffering from exposure or even hypothermia – this can happen even on a sunny beach or in a city centre. If you are in mountainous areas there are other risks such as frostbite.

The effects of cold weather can be exacerbated by:

● Windchill

- Rain and snow
- Getting wet and staying wet over a period of time (a long day sailing or kayaking can produce scenarios where people are wet for hours at a time. Add windchill to the mix and without drying off and getting properly warm serious problems can result)
- Insufficient or inadequate clothing
- Exhaustion
- Dehydration
- Poor morale
- Pre-existing illness/injury.

If you suspect hypothermia and medical help is a little way away you could use the procedure outlined below – you can use the same procedure for people who are just very cold and not exhibiting any other hypothermic symptoms such as cognitive impairment, confusion or other atypical behaviour – being aware of how members of your group behave normally can help in establishing atypical behaviour – get to know your group!

If you suspect hypothermia, call 999 for medical help. While you're waiting here's how to start warming someone through:

- Apply more clothing or an emergency survival bag immediately – these are usually bright orange polythene and available from all outdoor stores – they often have instructions printed on them for emergencies.
- Get inside.
- Remove wet and cold clothes and replace with dry clothes quickly – two layers of warm clothes will allow movement and skin to breathe.
- Use your body heat to help the warming process along or shield a casualty from wind and rain while a tent is being erected for example. Sit with your back to the weather and position the casualty to sit with their back to your chest, another member of your group can then sit facing the casualty and place his/her legs over yours and the casualty – hug together while shelter is made ready.
- A blanket or sleeping bag/duvet will help contain body heat – space blankets or survival bags are OK for a start when outdoors but can induce sweating after a period.
- Get them to drink a couple of warm cups of tea, hot chocolate or squash. A small amount of food is good, but too much can slow recovery as the body processes the carbohydrate – stick to liquids to start with.
- Allow extremities to warm gradually – encourage the casualty to move toes and fingers to stimulate gradual blood flow back into the limbs, but keep them under cover.

Remember, call for medical help the moment you suspect hypothermia or exposure.

Never:

- Use hand dryers to warm very cold fingers – this can actually inhibit recovery.
- Use hot baths or showers straight away after extreme cold – the sudden temperature change can inhibit recovery. This treatment should only be attempted by professional medics.
- Administer alcohol such as brandy. This raises the skin's temperature and makes you feel warm, while taking heat from the core – not good.
- Do anything that will draw heat from the body's core (the bit with all the important organs in it) to the extremities.

TOP TIP!

Keep an eye on the weather:

www.metoffice.gov.uk

Be ready to go to plan B if the weather changes suddenly.

We would rarely consider a nice hot sunny day as 'bad weather' but it can be just as harmful as cold weather if we underestimate the risks. Obviously sunburn is a risk that can have far reaching consequences, but heatstroke can be as big a risk, particularly when your party is involved in physical exertion such as a sporting event, a long hike or a long day out and about.

TOP TIP!

Make sure your pupils eat properly at mealtimes and drink enough water each day (2.5 litres is an adult's daily requirement). Then do what the Australians do:

- *Slip on a T-shirt*
- *Slap on a hat*
- *Slop on the sunscreen!*

Try to keep your party out of the sun during very hot parts of the day.

Command and control in hazardous areas

Hazardous areas are places where risk of injury or harm coming to your pupils is higher than what might normally be experienced day to day. Examples of such places might be the following:

- Lakes, riverbanks, bogs and marshes
- Coastal areas and cliffs
- Mountainous or moorland terrain
- Areas of ice and snow
- Busy road junctions
- Areas where large crowds might gather such as sports stadiums, concert arenas and busy railway stations or airports.

In places like these it can be pretty daunting to lead a party of children or young adults safely. What you need are command and control skills. In any of the situations above, you need to keep your party from harm while carrying on with your activity. But there is a fine line between bossing people around and taking command and providing control of a situation.

In a busy station leading a group of 30 year 5 pupils provides numerous challenges, not least keeping them all together and stopping them from wandering off to buy sweets, or trying your patience by hiding when you're trying to make progress. But then there is so much to catch the eye for a child and that, surely, is part of the charm of school trips. The classic 'snakes' that early years teachers use, where children hold hands and follow one teacher while another brings up the rear, might not be appropriate for those in year 5, so a more 'information and expectation' led approach is needed.

The reason that I use the word 'command' is that you should come across as 'being in command' and having 'authority'. In hazardous areas children and young adults need to know that they can trust someone to give good advice, make the right decisions and even tell them off when they step out of line.

Training for the outdoors

It is incumbent on your employer to ensure that the activities that the school offers are led by properly trained and experienced people. Training for your outdoor activity is a must you can't get away without it. Get training and get qualified.

Some local authorities provide training for outdoor education activities, but you're more likely to find training opportunities in the commercial sector. Go somewhere that is recognised by a national body and can provide a real qualification – take it seriously.

Apart from making sure that you tick the right boxes for any given activity, training courses that really stretch you mentally and physically are the most enjoyable by far. You make great friends and do something in common with the kids you teach – you learn. All of this provides you with a great sense of empathy for the people who learn in your lessons and gives you ideas for practical teaching scenarios in the classroom as well.

One-day courses are all well and good for an introduction to teaching or instructing an activity but are of no real practical benefit to you. Two-day or week-long residential courses are better for giving you an opportunity to really engage with the skills and knowledge required for what you are about to do.

Training courses for teacher leaders and helpers

Outdoor leadership

Summer mountain leadership training courses are typically a week long or more and then involve assessment over a further week. Alpine Ski Leader courses require training and assessment over six days on snow, while proper full-on instructor courses in mountaineering, skiing, rock climbing, sailing, canoeing and a range of other 'extreme sports' require much longer courses and high-level first aid qualification too.

If you're not taking kids into wild country but still want to learn about working in the outdoors with them, the Woodland Trust and other organisations like it run courses in teaching environmental education outside the classroom – ideal for key stage 2–4 and subjects like biology and geography. Other organisations run some super courses – ask your EVC or local authority adviser for help in sourcing them.

First aid courses

Two-day courses are the longest you can easily commit to. One-day courses only really provide the basic teaching in CPR and dealing with simple injuries. Get yourself on a two-day emergency first aid course.

Many companies will run courses tailored for the whole school staff, or to the specific environment you'll be working in – on water, mountains, etc.

Plan B – the escape route

Whether you are escaping from a bad situation or literally escaping from a hazardous area – when the weather turns nasty, for example – you need to have a plan B. The idea of a contingency plan was discussed earlier in the book, but when you are outdoors you need to have some sort of physical escape route planned that will get you to shelter, warmth and safety.

Young people on Duke of Edinburgh's Award expeditions know this all too well: it's part of their expedition planning process. When their route takes them over a hazard, like a mountainous walk or along a riverside path, they need to know a safe route away from the hazard that will lead them quickly to safety or to a form of communication like a road, dwelling or telephone box. We should do the same.

You can use the escape route idea metaphorically too, for learning situations: if an activity isn't going to plan, how can you escape that and bring your pupils' learning back on track?

Case study

Rachael's story

One of our Duke of Edinburgh's expedition groups didn't arrive.

Story told by Rachael, a senior school maths teacher and Duke of Edinburgh's expedition supervisor out in the hills with two colleagues and two groups of five 16 and 17-year-old students on their Gold training expedition.

> '*We were expecting to have seen both groups that day, on an unaccompanied section of their training route. Their routes took both groups over Pen-Y-Fan, the tallest mountain in the Brecon Beacons, from different directions so they should have passed each other. Although it was still daylight, the rain was coming sideways. We had six hours before it would start to get dark and we'd only seen one group. While six hours seems like a long time, it's not if it takes two hours to get down off the top of a mountain and set up in your campsite for the night.*'

Many teachers get involved in the Duke of Edinburgh's Award Scheme as part of their school's extra-curricular provision, while others volunteer for 'open centres' based in youth clubs and sports centres, or work as adult instructors in cadet organisations. Of course, some colleagues may never be involved in 'outdoor activities', but that doesn't mean that this story has no relevance to their contexts – there are many transferable leadership and management skills that we can learn from expedition leadership scenarios that apply equally to the classroom or a museum field trip.

> '*We normally organise things so that one of us drives a minibus and the other two walk the groups' routes towards them after being dropped off along the way. The idea is to have transport that can meet us at the end of one of the escape routes, and respond quickly to a phone call. We can't rely on the mobile signals, so we arrange meet points at certain times throughout the day.*
>
> *Group 2 had been over the top of Pen-Y-Fan where they'd had lunch and enjoyed the view before the rain came in. Simon, my colleague on the hill that day, had met them on his way up and had reported them to be in good spirits.*

He hadn't seen group 1 on his travels and assumed that they were ahead of him. He'd walked along their route, but had started where it began to climb the mountain hoping that he'd catch up with group 2 along the way. I'd done pretty much the same but the other way round.'

When supervision is done from a distance, as in this case, it is done because you want the young people to benefit from the opportunity to develop independence or team-working skills. Keay (2000) and Langmuir (1995) both give good advice regarding supervision and leadership of groups on mountains more generally – they're worth a thorough read if you are involved in or planning to be involved in outdoor activities and mountain walking.

TOP TIP!

Working efficiently as a team but being separated by many miles is a challenge that faces many teachers involved in expeditions and field trips. It is a type of practice that works very well and distributes skill, supervision and access to help over a large area, but it requires careful setting up. If you are going to work in a separated team you will need to:

- *Establish clear timings and meet points*
- *Share information – group contacts, medical details and parental contacts*
- *Have a good communication system*
- *Stick to a plan and set of protocols*
- *Agree all this before you start so that each person knows what the other is doing or will do.*

Rachael's story continues:

'I knew that group 2 had been to the top of Pen-Y-Fan before I met Simon there because they'd left a 'dead letterbox drop' for us on the cairn at the top. But there was nothing from group 1.

Dead letterbox drop

A dead letterbox drop is when you leave a note for someone you expect to be passing along the same route as you. It's a great way of communicating with groups when you are out and about in the countryside, as no matter how hard you try, getting to the same spot at the same time is pretty difficult, and if a group is trying to make progress you won't want to hold them up. Leaving a letter in a weatherproof wallet saying 'We made

→

THE CHALLENGE OF TRAVELLING WITH CHILDREN AND THE 'GREAT OUTDOORS'

it here at 14:15, we're all OK but the weather was light drizzle. We're now moving on to grid: 095 962 on a bearing of 240°' provides so much useful information and allows the group to communicate with you without being directly supervised.

However, you must take the message away with you when you go to avoid it becoming litter when the wind picks up. There is always a risk of it being stolen, of course – you'll have to take your chances, or maybe have a simple back-up plan such as a way of arranging rocks, or leaving a mark at the side of a path, to let you know all is well.

'It's not unusual for some groups to take their time, so we settled down for a spot of lunch and enjoyed the scenery despite the rain. The weather forecast wasn't too good for the late afternoon and we were keen to resolve the situation before too long in case things got nasty. We knew that Jane, who was driving the minibus, would be waiting at the end of our pre-arranged escape route and hopefully enjoying her lunch too, albeit in warmer surroundings. We'd planned that she should wait there until 6pm when she would drive to meet each group at their campsite and then drive to pick us up after.

Our plan was always to wait at checkpoints for at least half an hour before walking back down a route to search for a late group, so that's what we did. It takes a little bit of training not to let your mind wander and worry about late groups, because nine times out of ten they are just slower than you'd antici-pated and turn up in the end. We had a pretty good view of the surroundings but couldn't see anyone making their way towards us, not even that many other walkers. As we waited the weather got worse and worse and we were in danger of becoming cold and wet if we stayed on top of the mountain. We decided to move on.'

At this point, Rachael and Simon have no idea where the other group is and can't telephone them as their phones are turned off and sealed in plastic bags. There is no need to phone Jane yet as it's not close to 6pm, but if Rachael does decide to phone her she needs to be in a spot where she can get a mobile phone signal. They have clearly reached a point where they need to do something different in order to meet up with this group. But straying from an agreed checkpoint presents problems – you could easily pass each other by and miss each other by mere minutes. Nevertheless, at this stage there is no need to get worried.

Mobile phones and GPS devices on expeditions

In mountainous areas or areas with limited coverage these devices are only any good if they have a direct satellite connection. GPS devices work on this system but phones do not – they need a mobile phone tower to boost the signal up to a satellite.   →

The Duke of Edinburgh's Award Scheme recommends that young people do not rely on mobile phones and allow themselves to create a false sense of security. They need to be aware that their phones might not work. However, the scheme recognises that they are an important safety device that might be used in an emergency (if they work), so it would seem sensible to take them along, but ensure they are not used day to day.

DofE expedition leaders recommend sealing mobile phones with a fully charged battery in plastic bags using tape that you can write a date and time on. If, when the participants return, the tape has been removed or tampered with you know that they've been using their phones inappropriately. This is important for DofE expeditions as the participants should be independent of outside help throughout their expeditions. (See Keay, W. (2000: 421–423) for more on DofE and mobile phones.)

Getting help from the emergency services suggests that you've reached a point where you can no longer guarantee the safety of your group without assistance, and in Rachael's case that would mean not being able to find them. Missing a checkpoint is a serious problem, but it's not a good enough reason to call for help just yet. There could be any number of reasons for the late arrival of this group. They might have:

- Taken an alternative route due to fitness problems or ill health
- Taken a wrong turn and picked up their route further down the way
- Already been to the checkpoint and left a message that had been tampered with or stolen
- Already been to the checkpoint and forgotten to leave a message.

How do you make the decision to call for help?

Call for help when:

You lack the skill, confidence, expertise, manpower and facilities to bring about a satisfactory outcome to the problem in hand.

For example, if you suspect someone has a broken leg, you'd call an ambulance. If someone is missing, you'd methodically search for them until you reach a point where you've exhausted further options. But how long do you give it? Half an hour? An hour? Three? Well, that depends on the situation, environment, weather, hours of light left and the age of the child, young person or group. A DofE Bronze expedition group arriving two hours late is not that uncommon, but three hours? That's a bit much.

→

> **How do you make the decision to call for help? continued**
>
> If you are in any doubt, pick up the phone and call for professional help – it doesn't matter if it turns out to be a false alarm so long as you make the call in good faith and you've done things methodically first.
>
> Calling the emergency services is a last resort, but don't be afraid to do it if you have to. One of Langmuir's qualities of leadership mentioned earlier is the ability to make difficult decisions, and that requires good judgement (see Langmuir, 1995).

Rachael continues:

> 'I quickly sent a text message to Jane to keep her in the loop and Simon and I retraced our steps along the group's route. I went towards the start of their route and Simon went forward towards the end of it, just in case they'd passed us already. Don't forget that the rain was thrashing down and we wanted to get inside having found the group. Jane texted back and suggested that she drive to the end of the group's two escape routes. We agreed to give it an hour, so up to 4pm before we reassessed.'

Deciding on a cut-off time for reassessing is a good plan, but they don't want to leave it too long before they call for help, as any help would be hindered by the fading light in the evening.

> 'Simon's plan was to walk to the group's first escape route after the top of the mountain and see if he could see any sign of them along it. I did the same, but after an hour nothing turned up for either of us.'

Their method looks good – it's methodical and well thought out with clear deadlines – but now they reach another decision point. There is still no reason to be overly concerned as there is no evidence at this stage to suggest anything other than sloppy navigating by the group. Of course, leaving the checkpoint unmanned presents a problem. How do you know that if the group has gone off course, they haven't missed you in some sort of arc and arrived at the checkpoint after all? Another job for the 'dead letterbox', surely?

> 'Jane texted me to say that she'd been to both checkpoints and left 'dead letterbox' notes with clear instructions to break open the phones and get in touch. But she'd seen nothing of the group.
>
> 'Just as I was putting my phone away it rang twice and then stopped. It rang again a minute later and then it cut out as I answered it. Then a text message came through: "Hi miss wr ok sos we mssd u harry slpd & sprnd ankle we at

grd: 184 787." What timing! I think if we hadn't been able to get into contact on the mobiles we'd have had to call mountain rescue at that stage as the weather was poor and the night was not far off. Anyway, despite the poor punctuation I understood that Harry had sprained his ankle, on the way up and they were sitting tight. I hoped they'd got some shelter sorted. They must have gone off course on a different path up the mountain. I forwarded the message on to Jane and Simon and made my way to their position.'

Thank goodness for mobile phones – when they work! So, Rachael has knowledge of the whereabouts of both groups, and this is a boost to her confidence straight away. She and Simon must get there and assess the situation fully, but there are a couple of parts to the group's story that we already know:

- The group is stationary on a mountain in bad weather.
- One of the group has sustained an injury that needs assessing.
- It doesn't look like the group will make it to their campsite on time, if at all.

'By the time we got to the group at around 17.45, they were in pretty good spirits and Harry, the casualty, was sitting in his tent drinking hot chocolate. The kids had got the tent up and stuck Harry in it after they'd tried to carry on on what they thought was an easier route. When the rain came in sideways they decided to forget it and get some shelter. They'd picked a decent spot too, off the path, pretty sheltered and near running water.

Harry's injury looked painful but he was OK and had taken some ibuprofen and put a cold compress made from one of his wet socks, cooled in the stream. It was clear that he'd need help down the mountain though.'

Reflecting on practice

They've found the group; one of them is injured, sat in a tent drinking hot chocolate, but needs help off the mountain. It's going to get dark in two hours and the weather is awful. What would you do now?

(a) Get everyone organised to build a stretcher out of rucksacks and carry him down so you can all get to hot showers and the injured party off to casualty?

(b) Call for help: get the mountain rescue out and let them take over?

(c) Set up camp on the mountain and wait until morning?

Before you answer you must consider all of the possibilities and weigh up the pros and cons.

This is what happened in Rachael's story:

'Simon and I had a quick chat and agreed that the next course of action would be to stay put for the night, get the kids to put up tents, cook their food and stay warm and dry rather than risk a move down the mountain. We thought about calling the mountain rescue, but that would have meant putting them at an unnecessary risk as it got dark and the weather got worse. At least we'd all be OK in tents up here. Simon and I always carry small one-man tents with us just in case so we would be fine after a cup of tea and something to eat too.

We texted Jane with the details of what we were doing and instructions to call the non-emergency police number and tell them of our intentions and our possible need for assistance in the morning.

The police actually called back to check up on the call and make sure that we knew what we were doing – they seemed happy with the plan and had informed the mountain rescue people who would make arrangements for the morning. Simon, Jane and I were just pleased that we had some control over the situation again and that we'd kept everything together. Jane went off to the other group's campsite and we settled in for a rainy night on the mountain with the kids, who thought it a great adventure – far better than the walk they'd planned!'

This staff team have worked extremely well together and have shown superb judgement and a great awareness of their surroundings and the effect that their situation could have on other people. They've communicated well and shown a good deal of stamina in a challenging environment too. For just three people they've also been extremely effective over a large area. While they didn't find the group themselves, the systems and protocols they used for searching and communicating worked extremely well despite the limited phone coverage at times. Naturally, there was an element of luck involved, but also a considerable amount of skill, on the part of the young people they had trained.

We tend to forget that the children and young adults we teach can show remarkable initiative, skill and resilience to stress when they need to, and this must be due, at some level, to the example that we set them and the skills we teach them. Nevertheless, they deserve credit at times for the excellent way they deal with emergencies and difficult situations.

Conclusion

School trips require travel from place to place, and the more complex and challenging the method of travel, the greater the chance of something not going quite to plan. It's impossible to think of everything in a risk assessment, and critics of 'red tape' will claim that this is the weakness of a risk assessment in that everything you put on it is common sense and what goes wrong tends to be things you'd have trouble imagining. There is some truth in that, but the examples above do demonstrate that a good degree of forethought, planning and practice can make a difference. Whether it is getting you and your team to think 'as one' through protocols and systems, or training your pupils to react effectively to challenges, the work you do before you go can help you react more effectively to challenges you face when you're out there.

In Chapter 7 you will be invited to reflect on further challenges in two areas that often crop up when working with children and young people: injury/illness and behaviour. I've split these into medical and legal challenges, and while they aren't at the extreme end of the spectrum, they do represent serious scenarios that colleagues have experienced over the years.

Before you move on though, review what you've just read via the following key ideas.

Key ideas summary

- It's a cliché, but expect the unexpected when travelling with children and young adults.

- Appropriate training and reading will help your confidence, skills, ability and experience – being 'qualified' to do something means you'll do it well.

- Develop systems, such as the 'pyramid trickle-down' phone system or 'dead letterbox', to help you cope with unforeseen problems and changes to your plans.

- Trust your gut instincts and don't be afraid to assert your authority as leader and customer.

- Try to trust older children with more and more responsibility – supervise much less formally and expect more from them.

- Include older children in the planning process – seek their opinion (pupil voice).

- Consult your colleagues and agree the way forward.

- Use your school emergency contact – get them to work for you.

- Invite creative thinking to solve problems.

- Take advantage of extended networks of colleagues.

- Have a plan B, C and maybe even a plan D.

- Try to be decisive and creative but always think of the safety of your pupils and your staff and those you might come into contact with along the way.

Going further

Websites

www.dofe.org (The Duke of Edinburgh's Award Scheme)

www.pyp.co.uk (The national mountain centre Plas-Y-Brenin in North Wales)

www.sja.org.uk (St John Ambulance service for first aid training advice)

www.caa.co.uk (ATOL (Air Transport Operators Licensing) for information for air travellers)

Further reading

Cameron, N. (2002) *The Complete SAS Guide to Safe Travel* (London: Piatkus Books).

DfES (2002) *Handbook for Group Leaders* (Nottingham: DfES)

DfES (2002) *Standards for Adventure Part 2* (Nottingham: DfES)

DfES (1998) *Health and Safety of Pupils on Educational Visits* (Nottingham: DfES)

Keay, W. (2000) *Expedition Guide* (Wellingborough: Sterling Press).

Langmuir, E. (1995) *Mountaincraft and Leadership* (Edinburgh: Scottish Sports Council).

Relevant research studies

There is surprisingly little research into the way teachers adapt and adopt practice during field trips. What has been done has mostly focused on pedagogic practices rather than safety and group management and what teachers do when things don't go as planned. One helpful piece of research that looks into field trips is the 2008 OFSTED report on geography in schools. It's worth a read even if you're not a geography specialist as it deals with concerns that we all have about taking children out of the classroom.

OFSTED (2008) *Geography in Schools: Changing practice* (London: OFSTED).

Chapter

7

Legal and medical challenges for teachers on school trips

What this chapter will explore:

- Legal dilemmas
- Medical emergencies

In this chapter you will have a chance to reflect on a range of scenarios that focus on medical and legal dilemmas experienced by colleagues while on school trips. You will be invited to reflect on each problem via a number of prompts that may change for a given scenario. Travelling away from the relative safety and predictability of school surroundings presents a party leader with a number of potential headaches, many of which centre around medical problems or people's behaviour. Although behaviour has been dealt with elsewhere in this book, perhaps the ultimate manifestation of bad behaviour results in some sort of law being broken. If one of your pupils has been the victim of a crime, you have a responsibility to act and ensure their safety and security, just as a parent would. If the crime is committed against a pupil by another pupil in your charge, say theft for example, you can choose to deal with the matter 'in house', without involving the police. However, if a crime is committed against one of your pupils by a person or persons unknown to you, you must act in the pupil's best interests and this may mean involving the authorities.

Thankfully, it is rare that pupils on school trips are victims of crime, but it's wise to be prepared. Naturally you'll want to avoid destinations with high crime rates anyway.

Much more common on school trips are medical problems, even emergencies, ranging from the relatively mundane to the absolutely terrifying. Injuries and illnesses can really test your qualities of leadership and the robustness of your organisation. In this chapter you can explore these areas through the stories of teachers whose experiences have much to teach us.

Legal dilemmas

Know the law

As suggested earlier, it is vital that you have knowledge of some basic laws concerning your chosen activity. Whether it's driving a minibus or booking a long-haul coach trip, you'd be advised to have some knowledge of what you can and can't do. If you are travelling within the UK, you'll be aware of the law concerning drug use, smoking, drinking, drink-driving and what sort of behaviour might attract the attention of the police. If you're travelling overseas, the same laws might not apply – although the same or stricter expectations might exist regarding what is acceptable behaviour. Here are some suggestions in relation to the law overseas:

- Visit the Foreign and Commonwealth Office and British Council websites for travel details and advice about your destination (www.fco.gov.uk).
- Find out what the law is on smoking, drinking and drug taking. This doesn't mean you'll condone such activities, it just means you'll be better informed and more able to do your job.
- What about the law regarding your leadership of the trip? If a pupil is injured on your trip and you, the party leader, are found to be negligent in a subsequent inquiry, you could end up behind bars in some countries. The law at home and the law of your hosts both apply.

- Find out if there are any specific laws regarding your intended activity. If you are using instructors for adventurous sports, find out from the equivalent governing body in this country what the requirements are abroad.
- Know how you can get help abroad. Who do you need to call?
- Is there a consulate or embassy that you can access near your destination?
- Talk to people who've been before you.
- Read the guidebooks.

Respect local people and customs

Getting your pupils to respect local people and local customs is an excellent way of trying to avoid crime in the first place. By taking care not to upset people you can avoid misunderstandings that can lead to bigger problems. Sadly, some UK tourists abroad have earned an unhelpful reputation for being loud, loutish and drinking too much. Obviously, you won't be taking children or young adults abroad who can be described in the same way, but it is possible to be seen as guilty, just by association. Consider the following tips:

- Avoid crime hotspots.
- Tell your pupils to avoid wearing clothes that can cause offence such as football shirts, especially of national sides – they carry with them a history of dispute and fierce rivalry.
- Insist on excellent behaviour in public, especially during periods of free time – no gangs of your kids roaming streets.
- Know the local customs and what constitute offensive gestures or body language.
- Know a little of the language – please, thank you, excuse me, etc.
- Be seen to discipline any pupils who don't show the necessary respect to the environment, cultures and beliefs.
- Try to leave having made new friends – you'll be welcomed back.

Prevention is best

We all know that we can take measures to avoid becoming victims of crime. However, children are often delightfully naive of this so we need to educate them carefully. Here are some suggestions:

- Keep valuables in a safe place such as a hotel room safe – only take the cash you need for the day.

- Never advertise that you have money or valuable possessions.
- Don't allow expensive electronic items to be taken on your trip.
- Ensure that your pupils lock rooms when they are out of a hotel/B&B/hostel.
- Keep bags locked during flights or bus trips.
- Girls should be careful to keep handbags safe – wear them across the body. Boys should keep wallets in their front trouser pockets.
- Avoid dense crowds.

By taking these precautions you can reduce the temptation and opportunity for thieves to strike.

Victims of crime

Thankfully, younger children are rarely the victims of crime while on school trips because the teacher/pupil ratio tends to be much higher and supervision is constant and high profile. If anything, theft is the most likely crime committed and is more likely to occur within your party than from outside. It's tricky to deal with but ultimately has less of a negative impact than crime committed by strangers. Statistically speaking, we are most likely to be victims of petty theft abroad (if of any crime at all – it's still very unlikely), such as pick-pocketing or having a bag or mobile phone stolen from a café table, rather than anything more worrying. However, I've chosen a very unusual story that happened in this country, as it presents a number of interesting dilemmas for you to think about in terms of your own possible reactions.

Case study

Pierre's story

An evening's ice skating turned into a tactical retreat.

Story told by Pierre, a housemaster who took 25 of his boys, ranging in age from 13–18, ice skating for an evening with another male colleague, Nick.

'My colleague and I decided to treat the boys to an end of term trip one December, so we opted for a trip to an ice rink the evening before term ended. Most of our boys are boarders and live with us in a large boarding house on the school site. They are well behaved and polite lads who normally wouldn't get in trouble.

The kids were having a great time once we got going and seemed to enjoy me falling on my face on numerous occasions more than the →

skating itself. We'd been there for about half an hour and Nick noticed some of the younger lads were getting a bit of stick from some of the more experienced local boys, who were pretty skilful on the ice but seemed unsympathetic to beginners. Nick suggested a break for a drink to our lads and they came off the ice for a while.'

Removing the lads from harm's way should have gone a long way to ease the tension between the different groups of boys who were skating at different levels. Both Pierre and Nick were right to try to calm the scene but hadn't given any thought to the area they were visiting and the type of clientele the ice rink received on the night they visited. This was in the days before assessing risk was common practice. They'd naively assumed that it would be a straightforward trip into town, an assumption that proved optimistic.

'As the lads were queuing at the refreshments counter a couple of the younger boys got pushed out of the queue and told to leave because they weren't welcome as they were too posh! This didn't go down too well with some of our sixth form lads who were keen to wade in and sort the problem. We were even keener to avoid trouble so before too many verbal insults had been traded by well-meaning but foolish young men, we decided to cut our losses and leave.

As we were leaving to join our coach in the car park, a bottle landed at our feet and smashed, scaring the life out of us. It had been thrown by some of the boys from earlier on who had gathered to "wave" us off. We didn't want to appear spooked, so we got the lads to join the coach as calmly as possible.

When we started to board "all hell" was let loose. Three more bottles were thrown, landing on and around the coach, and as we boarded the local boys started to physically attack us and the coach. One threw a punch at Nick and two others ran ahead to try to get into the rear door of the coach. As the last of our lads were running up to the coach about ten local boys actually "squared up" to us and surrounded Nick and I before we could get to the coach, which was only about fifteen yards away now.'

Reflecting on practice

Wow! What a situation!

How would you react?

Pierre and Nick are faced with a scenario where running for it seems like the best option.

→

171

What would be your concerns?

Did all the boys leave the venue?

How would you suppress the situation and get away safely?

How can you be sure that you have all of your kids safely accounted for?

Pierre's story continues:

> *'There was nothing else to do than make a dash for it and clobber anyone that got in the way. So that's what we did, we got through by charging our way out, before getting to the coach as the driver pulled away. A couple more bottles landed on the coach windows before we were out of there and on our way home.*
>
> *As we sat on the coach and got our breath back after we'd done our most important headcount in all our years of teaching, we did start to wonder if we'd done the right thing. What if the kids had had knives?'*

This story does sound like something from the Wild West but, like all of these stories, is based on actual events – only details that would reveal identities and places have been changed. The strange and slightly sad aspect of this story is that it is not a wholly unique tale. The teachers here were faced with a number of complex dilemmas, not least of which was whether or not to use physical force against teenage boys in front of their own pupils and risk being charged with assault themselves by their assailants. But they didn't really consider their own safety either. This raises an important question about ensuring that leadership can continue. In a scenario where the leader risks their own safety unnecessarily, they can risk the success of the rest of the trip. Whether these two guys were right to stand their ground and then charge their way out is for you to decide.

Having got away from the situation they also have a number of duties to perform, which are common to any such altercation while away from home:

- Call your emergency contact and report the incident to school – take their advice.
- Call the non-emergency police number (i.e. not 999) and make a report of the events – do this whenever you witness or are threatened by violent acts in a public place. Get your report in first. Don't bother visiting a police station – get your pupils away and home or to a safe place.
- Record who did what and when as soon as possible, so that you have an accurate record of events.
- Keep calm.

It's difficult to say whether or not this sort of problem could have been prevented through any more thorough planning. Indeed, it was a test of the party leader's command and control and self-defence skills as much as anything else, but there are steps you can take to ensure that a destination is as safe as possible:

● Do the risk assessment with your specific destination in mind.
  - Consider the area and how safe you will feel with your pupils. Will you park close by or will you have to walk a distance? Any roads to cross or badly lit streets to walk down? What about service stations and stops along your route?
  - Talk to the venue manager – who else will be using the venue with you? A 'stag do' at the same paintballing venue may provide a headache or two. Has the venue ever experienced any trouble in the past?
  - Will bags or belongings be safe left on a minibus or coach?
  - Is there secure storage for coats and bags at the venue?
● Brief your pupils on any specific type of behaviour that might be best for your destination.
● Decide on an appropriate level of supervision for your trip and be able to adjust it as you need.
● Use headcounts and the buddy-buddy system when children are involved in an activity that is not directly supervised by you or your staff.
● Be observant and aware of what's going on around you.
● Communicate all the travel details and the itinerary to your emergency contact.

If the worst ever did happen and you or a pupil in your care becomes a victim of crime, no matter how petty, you'll feel helpless and aggrieved. The role of the party leader must be to maintain focus and try to show leadership by resolving the situation. You might be away from school but the support network and hierarchy still exists – use it.

If you or a child on your trip is a victim of crime at home or abroad, you should do the following:

● Establish a place of safety for the child.
● Establish and record the nature of the crime.

Acting in the place of the child's parents you need to try to do what you think they would do. At what point would you report a crime to the authorities? Should you just report all crimes?

● If the crime occurred in a hotel, shop, restaurant or somewhere similar you should report it to the management who will contact the police for you.

- If the crime happened in a public place you'll need to contact the police yourself.
- Report the crime to your school emergency contact. If it is serious enough your head teacher may want to get involved – don't be surprised at this, accept the help. Parents should be informed at this stage.
- In any dealings with the authorities you must act as your pupil's advocate and ensure their wellbeing and safety throughout.

On the other hand, if the law is broken by one of your own pupils you have a completely different set of challenges to deal with.

Criminal activity

I've deliberately chosen an example with a little more 'bite' than a story about a pupil stealing sweets from another pupil. Most of us have encountered relatively straightforward stories like this already and probably wouldn't be truly challenged by it. So the scenario that follows represents more complex challenges. Before you read on, it's worth pondering the statistics in the box below.

Did you know...?

'Two fifths (42%) of pupils had ever been offered any drugs, with boys more likely (44%) than girls (39%) to have been offered drugs. Likelihood of having been offered drugs increased substantially with age from 17% of 11 year olds to 65% of 15 year olds.'

Sample: 9,357 pupils from 285 schools in England in yrs 7–11

(Source: Boreham and Shaw, 2002)

Case study

David's story

We discovered drug taking on an overseas trip.

Story told by David, who took a diving trip to Greece with 18 students aged 13–16, and three other male members of staff.

'We smelt really strong aftershave on one of our lads every time he came back to the hotel after dinner each night. We were staying in a family run B&B hotel and ate dinner at a local restaurant each night, about a ten-minute walk from the hotel. We thought the lad had made friends →

with a local girl and fancied himself as a bit of a ladies' man or something. He was a pretty ordinary lad with a few friends on the trip so we were a little surprised that he kept arriving late. We like to give the older ones a little bit of free time after dinner as it makes them feel more adult. Anyway, we thought nothing of it until Kevin, a member of staff with us, reckoned he smelt something else one night.

It transpired after a very difficult chat with the lad that evening that he'd been smoking cannabis with one of the locals and was trying to mask the smell. We were surprised again because we didn't notice any change in his behaviour, but his roommates subsequently confessed that they thought he was acting a bit strange but didn't want to grass on him or cause trouble.'

Reflecting on practice

What are your options?

How would you establish the facts in this case? (See Appendices: Advice on interviewing children.)

How can you ensure that you do the right thing while protecting the interests of *all* your pupils?

What about this local? What's his role in all of this? Is he a supplier?

Do you involve the authorities?

David's story continues:

'We wanted to establish what role this local was playing in the whole story before we went any further. While my colleague Kevin and the lad stayed in the hotel lounge, we made discreet enquiries to our hotel owners to try to find out if they knew of any locals who might be selling cannabis. They'd heard nothing and the lad wasn't about to grass on his supplier. Our worst fear was that he'd brought it with him and that he might be stopped on the way home because of the scent on his clothes in his baggage. We were pretty sure that he'd not involved any other kids so decided not to pursue this local, even though he'd probably supplied the drug.'

In this case it looks like an isolated incident, but the teachers couldn't just leave it at a telling off and a confiscation of the pupil's drugs. Not pursuing the dealer is a sticky dilemma. He will have broken the law, and supplying to one of your pupils is very wrong. However, you run the risk of getting the boy into trouble with the police too. How can you do your duty and protect your pupil and do the right and legal thing at the same time? Answer: seek help.

> *'I couldn't conceal these events from the head, or just pretend it hadn't happened. We also had to take the best interests of the boy into consideration while thinking about the rest of the kids on the trip. Going completely by the book would have landed him in a police station, so we decided with the head's backing to destroy the drugs and make sure the boy's belongings were washed and that no trace could be detected when he flew home.*
>
> *We have a policy of offering addiction counselling to kids who first offend before we think of exclusion and we wanted to give the lad a chance. The head contacted the parents who agreed to our plan. We thought we did the best thing, all things considered. It meant more work for us – he had to check in with us every 30 minutes during the day when we weren't engaged in our activities.'*

You might argue for a different approach, but these teachers acted in the best interests of the pupil and did their best to minimise the risk of harm and distress to him and everyone else. They sought advice from senior staff and made a collaborative decision. But, *what if the pupil was accused of dealing drugs by a zealous member of the public?*

The answer to this question depends on where you are and the law of the land, how you interpret the school substance abuse policy (which all schools should have and make painfully explicit) and who caught them. 'Dealing' is very different from 'taking' and carries a possible custodial sentence in the UK depending on the drug and the circumstances.

First, if the pupil was caught by a private citizen then it is up to that person to inform you or inform the authorities – it is entirely up to them and you have no control over their decision, and nor should you. If caught by a member of the authorities (including police, airport security officers or officers acting on behalf of an aeroplane or ship's captain) then the matter is out of your hands – your role then becomes one of responsible adult liaising with legal representation depending on the definition of adult wherever you are. Schools might want to consider how they would assist in dealing with legal issues abroad and take a stance on defining who is responsible for providing legal assistance – parents or school – and when and where. The trip insurance policy will doubtless be essential reading here.

Let's imagine that you have been informed by the hotel owner and he has taken a tough stance on drug use in his hotel. You should treat this exactly as your head teacher would if it happened at school; follow the basic interview procedure (see Appendices) immediately, don't wait for the morning. If, after this procedure, you feel that an infringement of school policy and the local law has occurred then you should really inform the head teacher who can talk to the parents before you inform the police. Don't be afraid to wake the head up if you need to! The question of whether you should wait until you get home to deal with the issue does arise. You might feel you can make a 'judgement call' on this type of issue, but before you do consider where you are and your knowledge of the local law, or lack of it. In short, you need to consult with senior staff in the UK. If you take the wrong action and do not report an offence you could be charged yourself! Tread very carefully.

Schools and criminal proceedings against children in the UK

Schools have a duty to inform parents before taking any action that might involve the police. Schools can interview children without a parent being present (to try to establish the facts) but police in the UK can't interview any child under 17 without a parent being present. It may be different overseas!

Children under ten cannot be charged with a criminal offence. Children older than ten and under 18 can be, and would be dealt with by the youth justice system. (See: www.direct.gov.uk.)

If one of your pupils is accused of a crime by a member of the general public who wishes to press charges, you must continue to act in the child's best interests:

- If you think you can, try to calm the situation and deal with things like petty theft or damage to property by turning over the goods or paying up *but* only after you've established the truth of the matter and you think your pupil may be guilty. If you don't believe the accusation, or it's a more serious crime, you might have to submit to investigation by the police – you might not have any choice.
- Weigh up all the information before taking any action.
- Be your pupil's advocate – they are still in your charge and are still very deserving of your care.
- Call your emergency contact and take advice from the school.
- Get your travel firm rep involved to help if you are overseas.
- If abroad, contact your embassy or consulate for advice.
- Remember that police in the UK can't interview under 17s without a parent or responsible adult being present.
- Record everything you hear and are told.

It's highly unlikely that you'll ever have to deal with assault, theft or drug taking on a school trip in your career, but you do hear worse sounding anecdotes in school staffrooms. Wherever you go in the UK or further afield you can give yourself a great deal of comfort and peace of mind just by knowing how and where to get help if you need it. The same goes for dealing with problems that require a trip to hospital.

Medical emergencies

It is extremely unlikely that you'll ever have to deal with a real medical emergency on a school trip, but they do happen. Nosebleeds, headaches, stomach bugs, period pain, toothache, coughs and colds, and the odd broken bone are usually the worst you can expect to come across during your career. However, it makes sense to be aware of what you'd do if the very worst did happen. It's down to you to have a plan!

The newspapers are extremely reliable when it comes to reporting very bad news concerning children on school trips. It's terrible when the worst happens, and very often accidents that result in serious injury are genuinely hard to predict and build into your risk assessment. When things do go wrong, however, it is the teaching staff on the trip who can make all the difference to the outcome.

Plan for the worst

During your risk assessment planning meeting, you should give serious thought to planning for the worst-case scenario. If a protocol doesn't already exist in your school (and it really should) sit down and write one with your colleagues following your risk assessment meeting. In the few incidents where things have gone wrong, it has been knowing what to do next that has saved a trip and saved lives.

The protocol in the box below has been constructed to help to organise what to do in a number of different injury/illness scenarios. The colleagues who constructed this list (which has developed over the years) chose to use different levels to describe how serious a situation was. Following years of collective experience this is what they came up with.

> ### Note 4 (Protocol): Dealing with injury/illness/incident on your school trip
>
> Injuries are a reality when engaging in sports, outdoor activities and adventurous activities.
>
> The action of staff will depend on the level of the incident.
>
> In mountainous terrain the mountain rescue, ski patrol or police will manage the incident. If a hospital visit is necessary the party leader will liaise with ➔

Note 4 (Protocol): Dealing with injury/illness/incident on your school trip continued

the tour rep over visiting, transport, medical insurance and contacting school. The duty staff member will visit during the day if the injured party is hospitalised and ensure comfort and good spirits. *The duty staff member must stay in resort if an injured party is not fit to carry on with the trip activities.*

Levels of incident
(All injuries to be logged on pupil injury/illness sheets)

Level 1
Minor cuts/bruises/headaches and other aches and pains not requiring hospitalisation.

Action – party leader render first aid as required.

Level 2
Sprains, twists, injuries to thumbs and wrists, heatstroke, sunburn, dehydration, cuts requiring a dressing.

Action – see party leader or instructor in first instance, render first aid as required – ice and rest. May require a day off or trip to medical centre/casualty department.

Contact school if hospital visit.

Level 3
Any minor head injuries (i.e. not resulting in loss of consciousness), dislocation, suspected breaks, wounds requiring stitches, ice burns, frostbite, snow blindness, severe heatstroke, burns, severe dehydration.

Action – render first aid and transport to hospital; ambulance transport if no alternative.

Party leader to contact school emergency number to inform parents.

Level 4
Very serious, potentially life-threatening trauma, or critical medical condition such as, but not exclusively: significant loss of blood; exposure; hypothermia; suspected broken leg, pelvis, neck, skull; head wounds (i.e. heavy bleeding and/or loss of consciousness); appendicitis; meningitis; contagious diseases; malaria and others.

Action – call emergency services (999 UK, 911 USA, 112 EU); child to hospital as soon as possible.

Send staff member on duty straight to hospital with casualty and copy of emergency medical and contact details. →

> **Note 4 (Protocol): Dealing with injury/illness/incident on your school trip continued**
>
> Staff to contact school emergency contact – school will implement critical Incident Plan (CIP) under SMT direction.
>
> Staff action – Stop *all pupil based activity until safety can be assured*. Only resume after initial investigation of incident or after advice from school. If insufficient supervision is available return pupils to accommodation or transport (a safe place).
>
> Party leader begins to collect information and manage group. When group is safe, party leader departs to hospital, deputy leader remains with pupils in accommodation/transport (safe place). If insufficient supervision is available you may need to make arrangements for your party to stay with you.
>
> Appraise pupils of incident and ask all pupils and staff not to contact parents – the school will do this. Manage information to avoid stress and panic – reassure.
>
> Do not talk to the press.
>
> Do not contact parents directly.
>
> Follow advice from school/travel rep/medics.
>
> Always defer to party leader.
>
> (A less detailed form of the final part of this example can be seen in Chapter 4 on p106.)

In the protocol above, you'll note that the party leader does not automatically accompany a child to hospital. The reason for this stems from the need for the leader to lead the many rather than the few. Distributing leadership responsibility, capability and authority among a team of staff allows them to make the same or similar decisions as the party leader would in any given situation provided they're properly trained in the protocols. Once the party leader is happy that the bulk of the group are safe they can make arrangements to visit the hospital.

Of course, this protocol assumes that you have a good number of staff to work with. If you don't then you'll have to make suitable arrangements that work for you. Don't worry about supervision ratios changing if a member of staff has to accompany a child to hospital. Do the best you can but never leave the bulk of your group unattended unless there is absolutely no other way. However, *always do everything you can to ensure their safety*.

Here are some suggestions to help you prepare for injury and illness scenarios:

● Get some training – first aid courses are available commercially all over the country. Choose the course most suited to your type of trip.

- Know what you can and can't do as a first aider – can you give paracetamol to a child with a headache?
- Get together with colleagues to complete your risk assessment – what's the worst that could happen?
- Talk to colleagues who've dealt with illness and injury before – what worked?
- Get to know where the nearest A&E hospital is to your destination.
- Know where you can get help overseas.
- Produce a list of medical information for your party (adults too) – you'll want to know about allergies, current medication, previous illness or injury, next of kin details and who their GP is. All of this *voluntary* information should be shredded once the trip is over for data protection purposes.

Illness

The rapid spread across the globe of swine flu in 2009 meant that trips for some teachers and pupils were very different from what they'd expected. While this is an extreme example of a global reaction to a contagious disease and will probably rarely affect school trips, some stomach bugs can spread rapidly and bring a large number of people down with an illness in a matter of hours. The way that children interact with each other on school trips (in enclosed spaces like buses, planes, dorm rooms and minibuses) means that they are highly susceptible to airborne viral infections and diseases. You'll know this from how fast a cold spreads around even the largest school during the autumn term. One good thing to come out of the swine flu epidemic was that schools looked again at their critical incident plans (CIPs) in order to be prepared to deal with the problem.

Encouraging good personal hygiene on your trip can help eliminate some problems – when away from home, it's up to you to ensure that kids wash their hands and maintain their personal hygiene standards!

Accidents and injury

What do you have to do by law if there is an accident that causes injury on your trip? The straightforward answer is that you have to report through the channels that are in place in your school. You can do this through a generic accident report form, available from your school's health and safety officer, or you can design your own specific to your activity and get it approved. See Appendix 1 for an example.

Under the terms of RIDDOR (Reporting of Injuries, Diseases and Dangerous Occurrences Regulation 1995), your employer (not you) has an obligation to report serious incidents to the Health and Safety Executive (HSE) in the following circumstances.

- An employee or contractor:

1. has an accident that results in death or major injury (including as a result of violence);

2. has an accident (including acts of physical violence) which prevents the injured person from doing their normal work for more than three days.

- A pupil or visitor:

1. is killed *or is taken from the site of the accident to hospital*; and

2. the accident arises out of or in connection with work.

This second point includes:

- any school activity, on or off the school premises;
- the way a school activity has been organised and managed;
- the use of equipment, machinery or substances;
- the design or condition of the premises.

(See: www.teachernet.gov.uk/emergencies.)

So, if little Jimmy breaks his arm while skiing in the Alps on a school trip and goes to hospital, you should complete your incident report form, pass it on to the head teacher and he should inform the HSE.

Have a look at the scenarios described below and reflect on how you would cope. What protocols could you put into action? How prepared is your school for such problems?

Case study

Elizabeth's story

Our kids fell ill, one by one, over a period of two days – we were miles from home.

Story told by Elizabeth, a year 5 class teacher who took an adventure trip to Cornwall with 40 children and eight staff and helpers.

'Our little disaster happened when five staff, two mums and one dad took a group of year 5 children away on our annual activities camp. It normally lasts four days and includes all kinds of things that the children really enjoy like archery, canoeing, abseiling and raft building. We'd been at the activity centre in Cornwall for two days, having travelled down from our school north of Bristol. The kids were sleeping in really lovely dorm rooms in log cabins; about eight kids in each room with adults staying in chalets next to each cabin. The first day was →

great and finished with a BBQ in the evening and a sing song round a bonfire.

During the night one of the boys became ill, dizzy and a little disorientated; he was vomiting quite a lot and was really upset. We instantly thought of food poisoning but the staff were OK and we'd had no other complaints. The activity centre had a nurse in residence so we called her in and she took the little lad's temperature and suggested he had a fever and needed cooling down. We were worried that he couldn't keep any paracetamol down and we were always told not to give over the counter drugs to children anyway. By this time we'd called his mum who didn't drive and could only get down the next day when her sister could drive her. We "ummed and ah-ed" a little but decided that there was nothing better to do than pack him off to A&E with the nurse and a member of staff to get some professional help – we were worried that he might get worse and dehydrated.

Almost as soon as he'd gone, the floodgates opened. Most of the boys from our first little casualty's room started to show the same symptoms, and soon the place was like a scene from M*A*S*H. We got word from our colleague who'd reached hospital that it was probably the winter vomiting bug, even though it was nearly Easter. We were given some advice and kept the affected kids in their room. Problem was, we had another 32 kids to look after and ensure they didn't get ill. We couldn't take the ill children home, and if we had been contaminated after looking after the casualties my colleagues and I might've taken the whole trip down.

There was only one thing we could do really ...'

Reflecting on practice

What would you have done?

Does the story connect with your experiences?

Does it challenge you in any way?

How does it extend your thinking about your own practice?

How could the trip continue?

There are few things scarier for younger children than being ill and away from home. So, this story presents us with a number of dilemmas, not least of which is how to deal with the professional expectation that you should avoid touching pupils, given that you're going to need to reassure and comfort them. In this case, with children aged around nine or ten years old, how they handle being unwell will differ from child to child and across the genders.

To comfort these children, would you:

> pat them on the back?
>
> put a hand on their shoulder?
>
> sit on a bed and hold their hands?
>
> mop their brow to cool their fever?

Or would you feel uncomfortable doing any of the above? Don't forget, you're in a difficult situation: you are a responsible and caring adult away from home, but you're also a respected public figure, a member of the General Teaching Council and bound by a code of professional conduct. How do you get round it?

These teachers chose to follow their CIP.

'We phoned our emergency contact at school and got the parents to get in touch. When they rang we explained the situation and said that we had been caring for the kids the best way we could and had been holding hands or mopping brows and followed medical advice. We asked if it was OK to continue to do that.'

They did what they thought was right and made sure that their actions and intentions were transparent and appropriate. Good for them! But what about the other 32 children and five adults? It might have been easy to just call the whole thing off and all go home:

'We had to ask the mums and dads of the children who were ill to come and collect them. We'd discussed this in the original planning meeting but only expected it might ever happen to one or two kids. Each set of parents had a location map in the info we sent home, so that was one less headache for us.

We could have taken them all home by coach but we'd only booked it for the return journey at the end and the coach company weren't keen on transporting vomiting children anyway. The three of us who'd looked after the eight boys decided to stay clear of the rest of the group until we were sure that we were OK. I handed over leadership to one of my colleagues who already had a copy of all the important paperwork and we waited till the mums and dads turned up. The remaining 32 kids stayed well and enjoyed a great time, despite some being sad to say goodbye to their friends.'

A happy ending, but a tricky situation. The staff team were lucky to have sufficient numbers to be able to deal with this crisis and keep the trip running. Had they been further away from home, the situation may have been very different. What would you have done in France, Germany, the USA or even further afield? These teachers knew where to get help and how to resolve the situation because they were in their own country. If you're travelling overseas you need to know where and how to get help for children who fall ill. This should be one of the first questions you ask your travel rep or find out for yourself if you are doing your own travel organising.

Case study

James' story

Three of our kids were quarantined for a contagious disease. We were thousands of miles from home, didn't speak the local language and felt completely in the dark.

Story told by James, a secondary school geography teacher who travelled with 20 pupils and four staff.

'We had taken a party of 20 sixth form boys and girls on a cultural and geographical tour of mainland China. We were expecting to visit all of the top tourist attractions and some interesting geographical features along the way. Travelling by internal flights and coaches in between, we hoped to get as good an appreciation as we could of this vast country in the ten days we had available. The staff had all been on long-haul trips before but we had never been to China so opted for an organised tour provided by one of the commercial educational tour firms that colleagues from other schools had recommended. We were looking forward to meeting our appointed guide who was to be our interpreter for the trip.

Our kids had behaved superbly and the flight wasn't too bad although we were keen to stretch our legs and get to our hotel for a shower, some food and a better idea of what was ahead of us. As we got off the plane we marshalled our group through passport control but found that a second line of defence was in place. All the airport staff were wearing face masks and our kids were a little nervous of the situation. As we came through passport control everyone had their temperature taken with little infrared thermometer things. We'd been through this at Heathrow before we even checked in, so we were confident to move on. No such luck! Three of our students were refused further entry and ordered to be quarantined in a specially set aside hotel near the airport. None of them had exhibited symptoms of flu other than a high temperature, but there was nothing we could do. We couldn't visit them, reassure them or even stay in the same hotel. The only thing we →

could do was stand outside and wave every now and then to let them know we were there.

The worst thing was not really knowing whether our pupils had flu or not as the doctors could only release them once they were happy that they weren't infected. Meanwhile we had 17 sixth form pupils milling around our hotel worried that they were going to be next to be quarantined and that they'd miss a once in a lifetime trip.

The tour firm were great but wanted to know what we intended to do – carry on with the tour with the remainder of the party, leaving three kids and a member of staff behind, or stay put and miss all of our connecting flights and scrub the tour?

What could we do?'

Reflecting on practice

What would you have done?

How would you cope in a similar situation?

What would be your first course of action?

What protocol could you follow?

Can you deal with this yourself, or do you need guidance?

Who would you go to for assistance?

This situation raises questions about control being taken from you. In such a situation you would go through a range of different thought processes and emotions:

1. When children are hospitalised during a school trip you feel pretty helpless – there is often a long period of time between arrival and you knowing what is going on and this is extremely frustrating and worrying.
2. You feel somehow responsible although there was probably nothing you could have done to prevent it.
3. As a party leader, you've gone from a situation where you were in charge to being an observer.

How can you carry on?

How can you ensure the safety of all your pupils?

What about the travel plans? Carry on, or stay put?

With only ten days to carry on with an expensive trip involving connecting flights that might be at risk if they hung around too long, the group were torn between staying and leaving their friends behind. There was no sign that the three teenagers would be released from quarantine any time soon so they had to make a quick decision.

> 'We called home to our emergency contact and also called the British Embassy. Parents were contacted and able to call us. We agreed that we needed to carry on with the remaining 17 kids and leave two members of staff in a hotel close to the quarantined kids. The Embassy helped with a translator. A number of other school parties were in the same situation so some of the teachers from different English speaking schools were able to get together and talk through their dilemmas. We felt happier that there would be a little community of people "in the same boat" to relate to.'

Once the decision had been made to leave some of their party behind, the school contact was able to deal with the insurance implications back in the UK, leaving the staff to ensure that their pupils were safe and well looked after when they came out.

> 'We also arranged for some of our emergency cash to be left with the quarantine group and ensured that they had all the paperwork and travel documents they'd need. We then carried on with the trip – feeling pretty bad, I have to say, but there was nothing else for it.'

As with the previous example, this group were lucky that they had enough staff to be able to split the group safely and still maintain a good staff/pupil ratio. They took good advice and made contact with the right people. Thankfully, the three pupils were let out of quarantine and the insurance allowed them to join their friends later on along their route. Note that the party leader stayed with the main group and was confident in his team to distribute the leadership and care of the three kids left behind.

Would you have had the faith in yourself and your colleagues to be able to do the same?

Critical medical incidents

You can never be fully prepared for a really serious incident. When something goes very wrong, your heart beats faster in your chest and you breathlessly try to understand what's going on before you make a decision about action. Getting quickly from the moment of awareness to the moment of action without going to pieces requires some self-control.

Have a look at this more serious scenario below and reflect again on how you would cope. Try to think very specifically about trips you've been on or might be taking, and colleagues that you work with. How would your colleagues help? Can you visualise what you'd all be doing in similar circumstances?

Case study

Christine's story

We've dealt with kids sneaking booze on to trips before, but this time we were really tested by what happened.

Story told by Christine, who was leading a camping and navigation weekend trip with four colleagues and 32 year 10 pupils.

'We'd been taking a group of pupils out into the country for some navigation training in preparation for their Bronze Duke of Edinburgh's assessed expedition the following month. The weather had been good and the pupils were in a buoyant mood as they went to bed after cooking their own food, washing up and packing away their kit for the morning. The staff were camped in two tents: two male members of staff in one on the far side of the campsite and me and my female colleague on the side nearest the exit.

We'd chosen a site on the outskirts of the town where the school was situated as this was a practice trip and we felt that being close to home would keep costs down and enable us to make the most of the weekend before getting back to school.

After lights out at 10pm and a final headcount, we had some hot chocolate and patrolled the site, making sure that the kids were in their tents. A couple of the lads had escaped their tent to talk to some of the girls but were quickly herded back from whence they came and things started to settle down. As the evening wore on, we relaxed a little more and continued with the patrols every now and then until around 12am when we decided that all was quiet.

At around 2am we were woken by one of our male colleagues to hear that one of the girls was in a bad way in her tent. The girl was lying on her back close to a pool of vomit; she was breathing, but only in a shallow manner and wasn't responding to our shouts. An empty bottle of vodka was close by and the other girls in the tent had clearly also been drinking – they were panicked, hysterical, lacked coordination and couldn't be sure how much they'd all had to drink.'

Reflecting on practice

There might be a temptation to deal with drunkenness in a less than sympathetic manner due to its self-induced nature: 'They brought it on themselves, they'll sleep it off and be OK in the morning.' Maybe not – if the individual has drunk enough in one sitting, they can still sustain significant damage and, of course, can choke on vomit in their sleep. Treat an intoxicated person as a serious casualty who is at real risk of further injury or damage to their health. Don't let them sleep in a room on their own and check up on them regularly. In the case above, things are bad but could get worse

What would you do next?

Would you even have a plan for such an eventuality?

Heavier drinking among teenage girls is on the increase in the UK and the ease with which children appear to be able to obtain alcohol makes it difficult to combat.

Drinking in young people

'Historically, boys who drank consumed more units of alcohol in the last week than girls, although between 2000 and 2001 the difference in the amount of alcohol drunk decreased. In 2001 boys who drank consumed an average of 10.6 units compared with 8.9 units for girls.

The types of alcohol drunk have also changed over time – In 2001, beer, lager and cider were still the most common drink (drunk by 70% of drinkers in the last week), but prevalence of alcopops had increased in recent years to reach 68% of drinkers in 2001. The proportion of drinkers who had drunk spirits in the last week had increased from 35% in 1990 to 57% in 2001, whereas prevalence of drinking shandy, wine or fortified wine in the last week have decreased in recent years.'

Sample: 9,357 pupils from 285 schools in England in yrs 7–11

(Boreham and Shaw, 2002)

Drinking has always been a potential problem on senior school residential trips due largely to young people having an expectation of greater freedom when away from home. The problem is rare in primary education, but not unheard of. Drinking can also result in real life-threatening emergencies.

In this example, the teachers appear to have done everything right up to this point. They've positioned themselves carefully in the campsite, they've done headcounts and patrols late into the night, they've avoided booze themselves, they've caught escapees and returned them without fuss – and all after a busy day, teaching navigation and camping skills (in their own time, of course). On discovering the problem, the male staff have acted professionally and got a female member of staff on scene straight away. So there is no question of blaming them, is there? You might want to ask some questions about what happened before the trip left, however:

1. Were alcohol and drug policies and expectations made clear to pupils and parents in written and verbal form before they left?

2. Was a kit check carried out before pupils embarked on the trip?

3. Were any of the pupils flagged up for previous behaviour problems before the trip? Did the party leader check?

4. Was alcohol or drug abuse considered as part of the risk assessment?

5. Was a protocol decided upon for dealing with medical emergencies?

Assuming that all of the above questions can be answered satisfactorily, then we can fairly assume that this situation has come as a surprise and was not something for which they could have planned any better. However, there are a number of immediate concerns in this story that need dealing with straight away:

● In a small tent there is an unconscious casualty on her back with vomit close by, with three hysterical girls getting in the way.

● What if any other children had been drinking?

● Did the girls drink only one bottle?

● While not raining, it is cold and dark and people are tired.

● There are another 28 pupils who are becoming interested in what's going on.

How would you work through these challenges with your own team? What would be your priorities?

Christine's story continues:

> 'Steve, one of the male teachers, acted quickly to turn the casualty on to her side and into the recovery position so that any fluid could drain from her mouth if she vomited again. He'd checked her mouth for foreign bodies before he turned her and made sure she was still breathing. Jess, another colleague, got the remaining girls out of the tent, with sleeping bags and boots and took them over to the car park where our minibus was parked. I called 999.'

For a teacher it's a horrible feeling to have to dial 999 for one of their pupils. You can't help but feel entirely responsible. You might even momentarily question whether you should call for help at all, perhaps feeling that you've failed somehow and worried that you'll be blamed. Not so! If young people really want to find a way to misbehave or have accidents they will, no matter how stringent your control measures might be. Young people are resourceful and inventive and in normal circumstances you'd praise them for it. If you need help – get it!

'Our main worry of course was the unconscious girl in the tent. Steve was the most experienced first aider so he stayed with her while I called for help. David toured the rest of the group and luckily found no other drinkers, but discovered that the boys who snuck out of their tents earlier had slipped a bottle into the girls' tent and dared them to finish it. He dealt with them really well – he didn't shout or scream, but got the details quickly and got them up and dressed and made them make hot tea for the three girls in the bus and the staff in the cold, while we waited for the paramedics.'

Was that the right way of dealing with the boys responsible? I think so; better that they are busy and occupied with a task that might help in some small way to resolve the situation that they caused than shout and scream or leave them to 'do a runner'. Keeping them busy is good creative disciplining.

'The casualty got worse before the paramedics arrived, forcing Steve to help her to breath with 'mouth to mouth' at one stage. That was the only time that I was close to panic. I'd just been on the phone to our emergency contact to get her parents to meet us at the hospital and to get the other three girls and two boys picked up and taken home that night. Steve had been trying to get her to respond by scratching her feet and loudly calling her name and all of a sudden she stopped breathing. Thank God she started again! The paramedics arrived at the campsite car park and quickly took over while we gave details of her condition. All of this, from the start to when the ambulance arrived, happened in the space of about ten minutes.'

It's difficult to imagine what would go through your mind in such a situation, but luckily Christine and Steve reacted coolly and could rely on David and Jess to get on with the other necessary jobs.

'Jess and Steve went with the ambulance to the hospital to meet the girl's parents. They took the medical details file with them, just in case her parents couldn't get there in time and the medical staff needed more details. David and I stayed at the campsite and met the parents who had come to take home the three girls and two boys. We felt it best that their parents were responsible for their care as we were so close to home. All five were told to be in the headmistress' office by 9am on Monday morning. We still had a staff ratio of 1:14 so we were OK to carry on the next morning's activity.'

That is where Christine's story ended. The girl recovered although she had severe alcohol poisoning, requiring a number of unpleasant medical procedures, observation over 24 hours and tests on her liver function for some time after. All of the pupils concerned were excluded from school for a period of time and allowed back following their attendance at alcohol awareness sessions run by the school's counsellor.

Christine did the right thing by delegating the tasks around the group and sending two members of staff to hospital. One would have been fine, but she recognised the need for moral support. What about sleep though? If one of the four staff is expected to drive a minibus the next day we would want them to be well rested and alert. Ensuring that the driver had time to catch up on sleep would have been an important leadership decision.

This situation could have been much worse. If the casualty had not been spotted and put in the recovery position she could have been much more seriously ill, or worse. If the school emergency contact had not had access to contact details it could have taken far longer to get hold of the parents. The staff also used protocols to get things done by others back at school so that they could deal with the problem on the ground rather than worrying about making lots of phone calls and messing about with paperwork. The staff were clearly well trained and qualified and simply dealt with the situation as it arose without duplicating effort. They're the sort of people you'd want to work with.

Following an incident like this there should always be an investigation to clarify the facts rather than seek to blame. To help this process there are a number of things Christine and her colleagues would have been well advised to do:

- Record what happened and ask one other member of staff to do the same – do this independently. This is not a statement in the legal sense, just good honest practice, and it doesn't matter if you differ slightly in your recollection – it provides a form of authentication or 'triangulation' by looking at an event from a different viewpoint.

- Report to the senior management team – sooner rather than later when the memories are fresh.

- Suggest lessons learnt for the benefit of others – list all the things you wish you'd done. Pass this information on; it's not advertising a weakness, it's sharing experiences and it helps others.

- Identify any training that could have helped or might help in the future.

Why not try this?

You can find an example of an incident report form in Appendix 1 – feel free to adapt it to suit your needs.

Going to hospital with children

As I suggested earlier, there is nothing worse than having to take a child to hospital if something has happened to them on a school trip. You can't help but feel responsible – it's natural. Your role is straightforward in a way: you should act as the child's parents would if they were there. Naturally you'd do this while still maintaining a certain level of professionalism, but you shouldn't be afraid to hold a hand if it helps. If you have to go it might help to consider the following tips until the pupil's parents arrive:

- Act *entirely* in the best interests of the child.
- Ensure your pupil's safety. Hospital A&E waiting rooms can be pretty dodgy places at times – protect your pupil from harm or negative influences.
- Have medical information about the child to hand – either take it with you in hard copy or get someone to text you with any key facts (allergies, medication, etc.).
- Always carry important school telephone numbers with you on any school trip.
- Establish communications with your emergency contact at school.
- Keep your phone with you and 'on silent', but you should be able to be contacted by parents. Get the school to pass your mobile number to the parents who will meet you at the hospital.
- Take the names of any doctors who treat your pupil.
- Note down what the doctors tell you, keep a log of what's going on – it'll help you deal with long waits and make sure that the parents have all the information they need when they arrive.
- If things ever look like they are getting worrying, get a member of the school leadership team to join you if close by. If you're miles from anywhere get a colleague from your trip to come along if you can.
- Be prepared to make the right decision and take medical advice. If it gets to the point where a consent form is needed for a minor, you may have to act in the absence of parents – get them on the phone first though.
- Be calm and reassuring to all around you – you're the professional that your pupil needs to have faith in.
- Be prepared for the long haul – even a sprained ankle can take several hours to deal with.

When the child's parents arrive:

- Greet them professionally and introduce them to the medics who are dealing with their child.
- Be prepared for tears, blame and shock.

- Explain the circumstances surrounding the cause of the injury to their son/daughter.
- Pass on what you know – use your log to help you.
- Never say that you feel to blame, even if you do.
- Offer as much help as they need – never leave immediately.
- Only leave when the parents have had a chance to meet face to face with the medics treating their child.
- When you do leave, explain that the head teacher will be in touch soon to continue to offer support and answer any questions about the circumstances.

If you have to look after a child in hospital abroad, then you'll need to consider translators and daily visits. It may be unlikely that parents will be able to visit soon, if at all. If that's the case then duty staff visiting rotas and regular visits by the child's friends will need to be organised in order to ensure good care and the highest possible spirits.

Conclusion

A colleague who was kind enough to proofread an early draft of this chapter commented: 'Some of these dilemmas are a bit depressing aren't they? You're going to put people off taking school trips at all if they read this.' Worried that I'd just committed several thousand words to paper in vain, I reread the chapter and came to a more optimistic conclusion. The dilemmas aren't depressing at all, they are not scare stories; they're real stories that have happened to real teachers up and down the country. If you enjoy interacting with young people you'll want them to share your passion for learning, and that can't happen in only one place. You need to get out and experience what life has to offer. There are risks, sure, but we do our best to avoid them, and when something untoward crops up it is our skill, tenacity and wisdom that helps solve problems.

Knowing how colleagues have solved these problems and testing ourselves to reflect upon them is an essential part of our professional development that we ignore at our peril. Many excellent aspects of professional practice are borne out of just such a process of reflection and learning from the successes and failures of the past. In this last chapter we have explored some knotty issues that have hopefully provided you with much to think about in terms of your own professional practice. It is at this stage, then, that it is wise to ask one more time:

What have you **connected** with?

What has **challenged** you?

And:

What has **extended** your thinking/practice?

School trips and learning outside the classroom require dedicated and well-trained professionals who are keen to encourage and enthuse young learners about the world around them. Understanding the principles of good planning, organisation and leadership, and having a sound appreciation of how to deal with dilemmas, will help you to become the leader for learning that children and young adults need to inspire them and care for them when away from home.

Key ideas summary

- Plan for the worst – it will probably never happen, but you can never be sure.
- Get together with colleagues – talk about successes and disasters you've experienced and got through.
- Assess all the risks collaboratively.
- Know the basics – be prepared to get help if you need it.
- Your pupils' care and safety is your top priority – if they get in trouble you're there to be their advocate.
- Make the big decisions collaboratively, but have the faith in your leadership ability to be able to act quickly and independently if needed
- Have faith in your team and their skills.
- Share information – ensure that your colleagues can make decisions without you.
- Get protocols sorted before you go.
- Report all incidents accurately – use a special form to ensure you get all the information you need.
- Let common sense, experience and courtesy be your guides.
- Do what you feel is right.

Going further

Websites

For emergencies and critical incident plans (CIPs):

www.teachernet.gov.uk/emergencies

For travelling and the law:

www.fco.gov.uk

www.schooltravelforum.com

www.fitfortravel.nhs.uk

www.direct.gov.uk/en/CrimeJusticeAndTheLaw

For child protection:

www.teachernet.gov.uk/childprotection

Further reading

Berry, J. (2007) *Teachers' Legal Rights and Responsibilities: A Guide for Trainee Teachers and Those New to the Profession* (Hatfield: University of Hertfordshire Press).

FCO (2008) *Victims of Crime Abroad* (London: FCO Consular Directorate).

FCO and Lonely Planet (2006) *Travel Safe: Know before you go* (London: Lonely Planet).

Insley, K. (2008) *Teachers and the Law* (London: Institute of Education).

Ives, R., Ghelani, P. and Saffron, L. (1998) *Parents Guide to Drugs: What you should know* (London: Addaction).

Piven, J. and Borgenicht, D. (2000) *Worst Case Scenario Survival Book* (London: Chronicle).

Ruff, A. (2002) *Education Law: Text, Cases and Materials* (Oxford: Oxford University Press).

St. John Ambulance, St Andrew's Ambulance Association and British Red Cross Society (2009) *First Aid Manual: The Step by Step Guide for Everyone* (London: Penguin).

Relevant research studies

Boreham, R. and Shaw, A. (2002) *Drug Use, Smoking and Drinking among Young People in 2001* (London: HMSO).

Abbreviations

A2	General Certificate of Education – advanced level
AALA	Adventure Activities Licensing Authority
ABTA, ATOL	Association of British Travel Agents, Air Travel Organisers' Licensing
AfL	Assessment for learning
AQA	Assessment and Qualification Alliance
AS	General Certificate of Education – advanced subsidiary level
CIP	Critical incident plan
CPD	Continuing professional development
CRB	Criminal Records Bureau
DCSF	Department for Children, Schools and Families
DfEE	Department for Education and Employment
DfES	Department for Education and Science
DofE	Duke of Edinburgh's Award Scheme
EOtC	Education outside the classroom
EVC	Educational visits coordinator
GCSE	General Certificate of Secondary Education
GTC	General Teaching Council for England
HSC	Health and Safety Commission
HSE	Health and Safety Executive
IOL	Institute for Outdoor Learning
ITT	Initial teacher training
LA	Local authority
LOT	List of Travellers
LOtC	Learning outside the classroom
MIS	Management information system

MEd	Master of Education
NASUWT	National Association of School Masters and Union of Women Teachers
NQT	Newly qualified teacher
OFSTED	Office for Standards in Education
OSHL	Out of school hours learning
QTS	Qualified teacher status
STF	School Travel Forum
SMT	Senior management team
TDA	Teacher Development Agency
TES	Times Educational Supplement
TIC	Teacher In Charge
TLC	Teacher learning community
UK	United Kingdom of Great Britain and Northern Ireland
US/USA	United States of America

Appendix 1

SAMPLE FORMS

Trip organiser workbook example

Title of Trip Here

Sep-10

Pupils who've declared an interest in the trip/Initial nominal role

Record names and details as returned forms arrive

	Name	First Name	Yr/form	Tutor	sex	Deposit paid Y/N	DoB	Age in years	Dietary requirement	Allergies	Tetanus	Medication	Medical/other	SEN	Other? Behaviour etc.
1	Family name & initials	First Name	7		m	y									
2	Family name & initials	First Name	7		m	y									
3	Family name & initials	First Name	7		m	y									
4	Family name & initials	First Name	8		f	y									
5	Family name & initials	First Name	7		f	y									
6	Family name & initials	First Name	8		f	y									
7	Family name & initials	First Name	8		m	y									
8	Family name & initials	First Name	8		f	y									
9	Family name & initials	First Name	9		f	y									
10	Family name & initials	First Name	9		m	y									
11	Family name & initials	First Name	7		f	y									
12	Family name & initials	First Name	7		m	y									
13	Family name & initials	First Name	8		f	y									
14	Family name & initials	First Name	7		m	y									
15	Family name & initials	First Name	9		f	y									
16	Family name & initials	First Name	7		f	y									
17	Family name & initials	First Name	8		f	y									
18	Family name & initials	First Name	9		m	y									
19	Family name & initials	First Name	9		m	y									
20	Family name & initials	First Name	8		m	y									
21	Family name & initials	First Name	7		m	y									
22	Family name & initials	First Name	9		f	y									
23	Family name & initials	First Name	9		f	y									
24	Family name & initials	First Name	7		f	y									
25	Family name & initials	First Name	8		m	y									
26	Family name & initials	First Name	7		m	y									
27	Family name & initials	First Name	9		m	y									
28	Family name & initials	First Name	9		f	y									
29	Family name & initials	First Name	9		f	y									
30	Family name & initials	First Name	9		f	y									
31	Family name & initials	First Name	7		m	y									
32	Family name & initials	First Name	7		m	y									
33	Family name & initials	First Name	7		m	y									
34	Family name & initials	First Name	8		f	y									
35	Family name & initials	First Name	8		f	y									
36	Family name & initials	First Name	8		f	y									

36

Totals		
Female	18	
Male	18	
Staff Female	2	
Staff Male	2	
Total	40	

Staff
1 JHT
2 VM
3 PMG
4 IN

Note
Deposits and full amount will not be charged to those on Free School Meals. See policy on use of foundation fund for school trips.

200

School trip budget Sept 2010

This trip is an adventure holiday week and not covered by curriculum costs. It can therefore be charged to parents.

Trip Fund

		Price	No. of Pupils	Totals	Notes	
A	Cost per pupil (payable to school)	125	36	4500	Amount payable by school/foundation for subsidised pupils	£500
B	Cost per pupil (payable to 'Adventure Plus')	100	36	3600	Total to be paid to 'Adventure Plus'	
C	Drop-out deposits retained (£25 pp)	25		0		
	Number of 'free place' staff (1:10)		4	0		
D	*Difference contingency*			*900*		

Other costs paid from difference A–B

		Price	No of items	Totals	Notes
E	Coach transport (Acme Transport)	350	1	350	Coach is both ways and will not stop on site for the week.
F	Trip T-Shirt (School Kit Suppliers Ltd)	5	40	200	
G	Pay as you go SIM for teachers X 2	10	2	20	SIMs to be returned to office for later use by other trips.
	Emergency first aid kit	15	1	15	
H	Sub-total other costs			585	

		Price		Totals	Notes
I	*Remaining contingency*			*315*	Remaining contingency fund travels with party as cash.
J	Surplus from previous year's trip carried forward			75	This fund provides emergency cash to cover costs such as taxis, medication and other transport or replacement costs prior to an insurance claim.
	Contingency + surplus (I+J)			390	Some of the fund may also be used to pay for treats and other awards.
K	Extra adults/staff paying for selves	0		0	

Pupil and Parents' Contact Details

Title of Trip Here

Sep-10

#	Pupil Name	House	Form	DoB	Yr born	Age	Pupil mobile	Mother: First or second contact	Father: First or second contact	Notes
1	Family Name and initials	HS		18/11/1994	94	15		1		
	Family Name and initials	BBS		12/06/1992	92	17		1		
	Family Name and initials	RSH		16/09/1992	92	16		1		
	Family Name and initials	BBS		19/12/1992	92	17		1		
	Family Name and initials	RSH		03/12/1992	92	17		1	2	Parents overseas
	Family Name and initials	HS		28/05/1992	92	16		1	2	
	Family Name and initials	YT		08/04/1993	93	16		1	2	
	Family Name and initials	BBS		07/09/1994	94	15		1	2	
	Family Name and initials	SH		02/09/1994	94	15		1	2	
10	Family Name and initials	SH		13/09/1993	93	16		1	2	
	Family Name and initials	YT		08/05/1992	92	17		1	2	
	Family Name and initials	RSH		10/03/1993	93	16		1	2	
	Family Name and initials	RSH		29/06/1992	92	17		1	2	
	Family Name and initials	SH		16/11/1995	95	14		1	2	
	Family Name and initials	YT		21/07/1994	94	15		1	1	
	Family Name and initials	SH		28/09/1992	92	17		1		Lost Mum last year
	Family Name and initials	BBS		31/03/1993	93	16		1	2	
	Family Name and initials	BBS		10/12/1992	92	17		1	2	
	Family Name and initials	HS		09/07/1992	92	17		1	2	
20	Family Name and initials	HS		05/08/1994	94	15		1	2	
	Family Name and initials	YT		22/08/1996	96	13		1	1	
	Family Name and initials	BBS		04/10/1993	93	16		1	1	
	Family Name and initials	BBS		27/07/1995	95	14		1	2	
	Family Name and initials	RSH		27/07/1994	94	15		1	2	
	Family Name and initials	RSH		17/07/1993	93	16		1	2	
	Family Name and initials	SH		12/07/1993	93	16		1	2	Parents overseas
	Family Name and initials	HS		02/02/1995	95	14		1	2	
	Family Name and initials	YT		27/08/1996	96	13		1	2	
30	Family Name and initials	BBS		06/07/1995	95	14		1	2	
	Family Name and initials	SH		05/03/1996	96	13		1	2	
	Family Name and initials	RSH		21/06/1993	93	16		1	2	Father overseas
	Family Name and initials	RSH		15/05/1995	95	14		1	2	
	Family Name and initials	BBS		23/07/1993	93	16		1	2	
	Family Name and initials	SH		03/01/1996	96	13		1	2	
	Family Name and initials	YT		20/02/1995	95	14		1	2	
36	Family Name and initials	HS		24/03/1993	93	16		1	2	Father overseas

Pupil Details — Mother — Father — Guardian

Staff next of kin details

1	LHT	staff
2	VM	staff
3	PMG	staff
4	IN	staff

40 Total travelling

Note
Where mother and father are both shown as first contact this indicates a separation/divorce.

Reserves
6
Nemerov, ??? SH L5

Risk assessment form example

CONTEXT SPECIFIC RISK ASSESSMENT RECORD FORM School Trips and Educational Visits			
Name of School:		How many pupils involved and what age?	
Where is the trip/ event taking place?		When is the trip taking place?	
How will you get there?		Who will be leading the trip?	
Who completed this assessment?		When was the assessment completed?	
Who should read this assessment?		When should this assessment be reviewed?	

What Hazards might you encounter?	Who is at risk from the hazard?	How likely is Injury or illness? Low, Medium or High	What control measures already exist?	What additional control measures will need to be put in place? And by when?

Consent/acceptance form example

School Name and Address

Tour/trip/excursion to: .... **Dates from** .... **to** ....

Teacher IC ....

I have read the information provided by the organiser/leader of this tour/trip/excursion and I understand that this forms the basis of a contract between (School Name) and the parents of:

_____ (Full Name)

I, and my son/daughter/(s) agree that he/she/they will abide by the Code of Conduct and we accept the rules, regulations, terms and conditions set out by (School Name) for the trip/ activity.

I agree that he/she/they may take part in all activities, which form part of the trip and that he/she/they will follow the instructions of members of staff or other adult supervisors and instructors. I give consent for my child/children to take part in winter sports activities as outlined in the details aforementioned.

I agree that the organiser/leader or the senior member of staff present may authorise any emergency medical treatment, including an operation or the administration of an anaesthetic, should it be considered necessary, if it is impossible to obtain parental permission speedily enough.

Signed _____ Parent/Guardian

Name _____ (Please print)

Signed _____ Pupil

Name _____ (Please print)

Date _____

FAMILY CONTACT ADDRESSES AND TELEPHONE NUMBERS

Dates:	Address: _____	Dates:	Address: _____
From: _____	_____	From: _____	_____
To: _____	_____	To: _____	_____
	Phone: _____		Phone: _____

PLEASE GIVE THE NAME AND ADDRESS OF A RELATIVE/FRIEND WHO COULD BE CONTACTED IN THE EVENT OF CONTACT NOT BEING MADE WITH YOU.

Dates:	Address: _____	Dates:	Address: _____
From: _____	_____	From: _____	_____
To: _____	_____	To: _____	_____
	Phone: _____		Phone: _____

When completed, please return this form to the lead teacher as stated above. Please ensure the whole form is completed including the contact dates, addresses and telephone numbers requested above.

Staffroom noticeboard trip list example

Design & Technology Product Design Seminar
University of London
Monday 7th December
Leave: 08.30
Return to School: 18:00
Travel: Train and tube
Staff: JHT

The sixth form students listed here will be joining me on a trip
to the Institute of Education. Please accept my apologies for
any disruption this may cause to your planned lessons on
Monday.

Full details are posted in the school reception.

I have asked that work is caught up in a suitably timely
manner.

JHT

Contact Information
JHT: 07789******
Training Partnership: 01727 ******

Institute of Education: 020 7612 6000

CHUNG, Simon	FIELD, David J.
COLLIAS, Christian A.	FLOOD, Edmund M. W.
FRANCEY, Alastair W.	HATHAWAY, Ethan J.
GRAY, Stuart J. A	RADTKE, Phillip
HARRIS, Thomas J.	RINGEL, Christopher F.
NEWTON, Felicity A.	STUBBS, Carys A.
WARNER, Natalie C.	ZILKENS, Andre
COLLINS, Paul S.	

Pupil injury/illness/incident record form example

School Name and Address

Pupil Injury/Illness/Incident Record Form

Name of pupil: _____ **Date of incident** _____

Place and time _____

Name of instructor/teacher present: _____ Member of staff on duty: _____

Paramedic involved?   NO   YES   ID no: _____

Police or rescue services involved?   NO   YES   ID no: _____

First aid administered?   NO   YES   By whom: _____

College contacted?   NO   YES   date _____ time _____

Third party involved?   NO   YES

Third party name and address

```
┌──────────────────────────────────────────────────────────────┐
│                                                                │
│                                                                │
└──────────────────────────────────────────────────────────────┘
```

Brief description of incident (include evacuation details) continue on back of sheet if necessary.

```
┌──────────────────────────────────────────────────────────────┐
│                                                                │
│                                                                │
│                                                                │
│                                                                │
│                                                                │
└──────────────────────────────────────────────────────────────┘
```

Treatment

Hospital _____ Doctor attending: _____

Initial diagnosis _____

Prescription issued? _____

Family doctor? _____

Action on return home/school

```
┌──────────────────────────────────────────────────────────────┐
│                                                                │
│                                                                │
│                                                                │
└──────────────────────────────────────────────────────────────┘
```

This form completed by:

Print _____ Sign _____ Date _____

Position (party leader/assistant teacher, etc.): _____

Pupil medical details declaration form example

School Name and Address

School Trip Medical Declaration Form

Your name _____ Date of birth _____

Today's date _____

Date of last tetanus if known

Allergies (e.g. Penicillin, nuts or other foods)

Known medical conditions (e.g. Asthma)

Any specific injuries that could effect your health (e.g. recent breaks, damaged muscles, tendons, ligaments, etc)

You do not have to give the following information but it may be helpful in the event of ill health
Are you currently taking prescription medicine?   **Yes   No**

Type of medicine? _____

The information you have given above will remain strictly confidential and will only be used to assist you in the event of an injury or ill health.

Appendix 2

ADVICE ON INTERVIEWING CHILDREN WHEN AWAY FROM HOME

Basic interview procedure

Assuming that you can't contact a senior member of staff immediately, you must assume this role. There is no time for prevarication. You're the professional on the spot.

You must interview immediately for a number of reasons. Mobile phones make contacting others, maybe parents, very easy, even from the most far-flung corners of the world. An emotional phone call home to parents can distort the facts and make things difficult to recall with clarity. Also, time to think about a problem can lessen its importance or blow it out of proportion – neither is helpful.

Interviewing the accuser/victim

Stick to questions that will get facts and don't put words into people's mouths. Ensure that this person feels supported and right to raise concerns.

Use this format to help:

Reassure, Establish, Explain, Reassure again

Remember that you are dealing with children for whom you are responsible, even the wrongdoer.

It is also important to remember that just because somebody accuses someone of something it does not mean that what you hear is true. Be prepared to listen to everyone's side of the story.

1. **Reassure**:
   - Interview the accuser/victim with another member of staff present and taking notes.
   - Inform the accuser/victim that this information cannot remain confidential between you and may need to be reported to the head teacher or appropriate authorities (if of a sufficiently serious nature, say drugs, assault, alcohol, bullying), but that you will do your best to ensure this is done with the utmost discretion and with their safety and happiness in mind.

2. **Establish**:
   - **Who**? The alleged offender(s), name and/or description. (Do this first so a member of staff can contact the accused.)
   - **What**? What happened and how?
   - **Where**?
   - **When**?
   - **Safety**. Has/is anyone been/being harmed?
   - **Evidence**. Does any exist? (Appoint a member of the staff team to collect this.)
   - **Witnesses**. Are there any?
   - **Confidentiality**. Has the accuser/victim spoken to anyone else regarding this issue?

3. **Explain**:
   - Exactly what will happen in terms of the investigation and how you will tackle it.
   - Explain what you understand to have happened.

4. **Reassure again**:
   - Ask the accuser/victim to wait in a place of safety with friends and a member of your staff team, or a responsible pupil, while the rest of the investigation is carried out.

Interviewing the accused

Allow time to consult with your assistant and clarify the notes that they have taken. Do you agree on what you have heard? Don't start this second interview without being clear on what you have heard in the first.

You must try to remain impartial; remember that you have the accused's wellbeing to consider too, and you may have to be their advocate if things go further. Once again, you are in a position of *loco parentis* and must act accordingly.

Reassure, Establish, Explain, Reassure again

1. **Reassure**:
   - Interview the accused with another member of staff present and taking notes.
   - Explain that you have a concern and you need the accused to tell the truth. Make sure that they know that you have their safety and best interests at heart and will do your utmost to support them.
   - Do not, at this or any other stage, accuse the individual of anything at all. You are trying to establish their side of the story, not achieve a 'conviction'.
   - Try to gain trust.

2. **Establish:**
   - **What?** What were the accused's activities when the alleged event(s) took place? Record the 'facts' that you have been able to ascertain – things that link to the previous interview with the accuser/victim. Highlight any of the inconsistencies to the accused and ask for further explanation.
   - **Where?** Look for matching places.
   - **When?** Look for matching times.
   - **Evidence.** Does any exist that might help?
   - **Witnesses.** Are there any?
   - **Confidentiality.** Has the accused spoken to anyone else regarding this issue?

3. **Explain:**
   - Explain that an accusation against them has been made. Ask if they know what it might be about. Give every opportunity for the accused to talk and have a say, do not interrupt. Let them finish speaking when they want to.
   - Explain what you understand to be the accused's version of events and what you will do next (see below).

4. **Reassure again:**
   - Ask the accused to wait in a place of safety with a member of your staff team or a responsible senior pupil while the rest of the investigation is carried out. Give them an opportunity to change their story if they feel it does not match up. Avoid asking them to write a signed statement. Do not pass judgement at this stage.

Note that it is important to exercise caution here as a runaway child in fear of persecution is a situation you want to avoid. Explain that they can talk to you at any time and that the interview cannot remain confidential but will be treated with discretion and that they will continue to receive support from you and your staff during the trip.

The above assumes that your accused is a willing participant on getting to the truth. If they are not then you may have a bigger problem. You can't ignore problems but you must try to avoid confrontation – you don't want a pupil 'doing a runner'. If you can't find the accused pupil you must act as if that person is missing in the first instance. As a general rule I would inform the authorities if a mealtime or agreed meeting time is missed by more than an hour.

What now? Decision time …

Following the interviews you must meet with your staff team. Leadership needn't be a lonely role. Lay out the information that you have. Ask for comment. Consider the views of your team and suggest a course of action. If you all think that someone is lying then that is fine; don't be afraid of this but be very careful how you phrase it. Whether it is the accuser/victim or the accused, it's often best just to say that accounts conflict. Be prepared to justify your decisions to anyone, and stick by them. Record your conversation and your recommended course of action. Then take it. This may mean informing external authorities or the head teacher instantly.

How long should the interview process take?

The process should take no more than half an hour – try to act immediately but without fuss. Be calm and professional. If there is a serious allegation you could cause problems by taking longer than this.

Multiple interviews

You may have to interview a number of pupils in order to get to the bottom of things. How many depends entirely on the nature of the occurrence. The above procedure should give you a framework within which to work and is a good basis for remaining impartial. If it works for you then adopt it; if not, adapt it for your own needs. In my experience these things do happen and the better prepared for them you are the calmer and more impartial, and therefore effective, you can be.

Appendix 3

MORE CHALLENGING SCENARIOS

We have been asked to take children away who are on medication for depression. Is this right and fair on us and the rest of the children?

One of my sixth formers wanted permission to take a train journey from our ski resort to visit friends in Vienna for a day or two 'whilst he was in the area' – his mum had given him permission.

Four of our girls had been intimidating another pupil with constant verbal digs whenever the staff weren't around. We didn't know about it until he burst into tears on the penultimate day of our trip. How could we have prevented this?

We thought everyone was on the train until we did a 'double-check' headcount and found that we'd lost one boy – just as we were pulling out of the station – in Paris.

One of our girls was refused entry into the country; they say she'll have to get the next flight home.

One of my members of staff has been keeping the sixth form out drinking late into the night and refuses to listen to my requests to follow our agreed rules on drinking and staff/pupil interaction. He says it doesn't count on school trips abroad, it's part of growing up for the kids.

We'd travelled a long way to do some biology fieldwork on the island of Flat Holm in the Bristol Channel – all went well during our three-day stay until the seas got rough ... we were stranded for two more days.

I overheard some of the pupils talking about a relationship between one of the sixth form boys and a young female member of staff on my trip. I have no concrete evidence as such, but I've started to notice that the teacher acts differently around the boy. We've got five days left of our trip. What do I do now?

My heart skipped a beat when one of our pupils was taken away behind a screen at the X-ray baggage check by security at the airport. We weren't even contacted despite telling the airport beforehand that we were a school party.

Our classes are 30-plus kids in some cases and we can't afford the lesson cover so that we can take whole classes of school trips. We can't use parents to help supervise because the head says we need to CRB check them, and we've just lost three classroom assistants through redundancy because of education cuts. What do we do now?

We used to run some excellent language exchanges at the school in French and German. The pupils stay with host families for a week when we go overseas, but we can't ask our own parents to host our French or German pupils because we would have to CRB check them all. We just can't afford it! How can we continue to offer high quality language experiences when our kids can't be involved in an exchange? Exchanges can't work in just one direction. It's bad enough that national uptake of our subject at GCSE is less than it was in 1998. Where do we go from here?

Index

Classroom Gems

Innovative resources, inspiring creativity across the school curriculum

Designed with busy teachers in mind, the Classroom Gems series draws together an extensive selection of practical, tried-and-tested, off-the-shelf ideas, games and activities, guaranteed to transform any lesson or classroom in an instant.

Games and activities for
Primary Modern Foreign Languages
Nexxo Drinkwater

© 2008 Paperback 336pp
ISBN: 9781405873925

Practical ideas, games and activities for the
Primary Classroom
Paul Barron

© 2008 Paperback 312pp
ISBN: 9781405859455

Games, ideas and activities for
Primary PE
Will Allen

© 2009 Paperback 224pp
ISBN: 9781408220382

Games, ideas and activities for
Learning Outside the Primary Classroom
Paul Bomphrey

© 2009 Paperback 256pp
ISBN: 9781408225608

Games, ideas and activities for
Primary Mathematics
John Dabell

© 2009 Paperback 304pp
ISBN: 9781408223208

Games, ideas and activities for
Primary Humanities
Richard Green

© 2009 Paperback 304pp
ISBN: 9781408228098

Games, ideas and activities for
Primary Music
Donna Minto

© 2009 Paperback 304pp
ISBN: 9781408223260

Games, ideas and activities for
Primary Drama
Michael Theodorou

© 2009 Paperback 304pp
ISBN: 9781408223291

Games, ideas and activities for
Early Years Phonics
Lynn Cousins and Gill Coulson

© 2009 Paperback 304pp
ISBN: 9781408224359

Creative activities for the
Secondary Classroom
Mark Labrow

© 2009 Paperback 256pp
ISBN: 9781408225578

Games, ideas and activities for
Primary Science
John Dabell

© 2010 Paperback 304pp
ISBN: 9781408223239

Games, ideas and activities for
Primary Literacy
Hazel Glynne and Amanda Snowden

© 2010 Paperback 336pp
ISBN: 9781408225516

'Easily navigable, allowing teachers to choose the right activity quickly and easily, these invaluable resources are guaranteed to save time and are a must-have tool to plan, prepare and deliver first-rate lessons'

The Essential Guides Series

Practical skills for teachers

The Essential Guides series offers a wealth of practical support, inspiration and guidance for NQTs and more experienced teachers ready to implement into their classroom. The books provide practical advice and tips on the core aspects of teaching and everyday classroom issues, such as planning, assessment, behaviour and ICT. The Essential Guides are invaluable resources that will help teachers to successfully navigate the challenges of the profession.

The Essential Guide to
Secondary Teaching
Susan Davies
© 2010 paperback
ISBN 978-1-4082-2452-6

The Essential Guide to
Using ICT Creatively in the Primary Classroom
Steve Woods
© 2010 paperback
ISBN 978-1-4082-2497-7

The Essential Guide to
Taking Care of Behaviour
(second edition)
Paul Dix
© 2010 paperback
ISBN 978-1-4082-2554-7

The Essential Guide to
Classroom Assessment
Paul Dix
© 2010 paperback
ISBN 978-1-4082-3025-1

The Essential Guide to
Understanding Special Educational Needs
Jenny Thompson
© 2010 paperback
ISBN 978-1-4082-2500-4

The Essential Guide to
Shaping Children's Behaviour in the Early Years
Lynn Cousins
© 2010 paperback
ISBN 978-1-4082-2502-8

The Essential Guide to
Teaching 14-19 Diplomas
Lynn Senior
© 2010 paperback
ISBN 978-1-4082-2549-3

Longman is an imprint of

PEARSON

Practical skills for teachers